TAKING THE PLUNGE

For

Thataw, Chitlu and Leysay,

Karen friends from Burma

TAKING THE PLUNGE

SEEKING ACCOMPANYING BAPTISING

WIPF & STOCK · Eugene, Oregon

TAKING THE PLUNGE
Seeking, Accompanying, Baptising

Wipf & Stock
An Imprint of Wipf and Stock Publishers
199 W. 8th Ave., Suite 3
Eugene, OR 97401

www.wipfandstock.com

ISBN 13: 978-1-60899-922-4

First published in Australia in 2008
By Spectrum Publications Pty Ltd
PO Box 75, Richmond, Vic Australia 3121

Photos:
The greyscale at the beginning of each section is a depiction of the Women at the Well (John 4) entitled Water of Life by the sculptor Steven Broadbent, Chester Cathedral. Used with permission.

Manufactured in the U.S.A.

CONTENTS

FOREWORD

This book is the product of nine years of creative engagement of a parish community with those on its edge. The enterprise had a leadership team consisting of different individuals over those years. Their dedication was in the form of an openness of sharing and listening together with inquirers in order to find the way into a living faith.

They were exciting years. The parish was Williamstown, a suburb of Melbourne. When I left that parish I set sail on the task of reflecting on the historical roots of the journey approach used and also on some of the elements of western culture that became manifest in the process.

This book is about the outcomes of the so-called 'Easter Journey' process that was the focus of those nine years. Rather than tracing a local story, those years provide the necessary background for the four sections that make up the book. As I point out in the following pages this book is not a 'how to' manual about this inter-active, non-curriculum based approach. Others have written about that. The suggested outcomes of the process, however, both immediate – and long-term, have not been written about in a deliberate manner. The question of what this way of initiation means for the future of the Church in the West is, I believe, becoming critically important.

My thanks are to those who introduced me to the 'Easter Journey' or catechumenal process – especially to my Anglican colleague Paul Dalzell who mentored me through my first facilitation of it. That year, 1996, was the first of those several years in the Anglican parish of Williamstown in which with others we pioneered a local expression of the process. I am grateful to both the fellow clergy serving in the parish at that time and to the lay people – with whom I shared the leadership. Many people benefited from those years of faith and community discovery including ourselves.

The Rite of Christian Initiation of Adults (RCIA) within the Roman Catholic Church has continued to be an inspiration to me and others who adopt a journey focus with regard to outreach and initiation. The enthusiasm of some American Episcopalians, especially Steve Zimmerman of Florida, in relation to the Catechumenate, has also urged me on.

St Deiniol's Library in Wales kindly provided me with a month-long residential scholarship to do research and lay out the task at hand. The Australian Research Theological Foundation and the Society of the Sacred Mission each enabled me to set aside time for writing the manuscript.

Throughout the writing period I intended this book to have a thoroughly ecumenical pitch. Hence I wanted the readers of the draft to be from various main-stream church traditions. I thank the readers, Bob Dixon, Janet Howie, Bishop Bill Ray, Jeanette Acland and Adrian Evans, for their helpful comments that improved areas of the text. I also am grateful to Associate Professor Gerald Moore of the Sydney College of Divinity for his positive remarks that have supported publication.

INTRODUCTION

A great exponent of the need to find meaning within the height and depth of the human journey is the writer Paulo Coelho, most popular for his book, *The Alchemist*. He provides avenues of wisdom for life's journey. To many, especially young people, he exemplifies powerfully the challenge and excitement with regard to seeking and searching.

"I look at life, using the metaphor of the journey, as a caravan: I know neither whence it came nor where it's going."[1] For him the journey and caravan of life is all about exploration of meaning and purpose. His own 'caravan' has travelled through times of prison and torture. It has included delving into black magic (a time of deep despair) and being subject to mental illness. His biographer writes of this period of his life, "Coelho was a nonconformist, a seeker after the new, leading him to try everything good and bad that appeared along the way."[2] For a time he was a successful actor. After three failed marriages he met Christina, a painter, and became happily married. In 1981 they travelled extensively and while in Germany visited a concentration camp. Responding to what he encountered he underwent a profound spiritual experience, such that he decided to return to the Catholic faith of his childhood. Walking the Spanish pilgrimage route to Santiago de Compostela confirmed him in his new-found direction.

Coelho's own life represents *every-person* as a wanderer and seeker, albeit dramatically. All of us have rich experiences which we need to discover the significance of and see what they mean for the whole of our lives.

How can those, whom I am calling wanderers or seekers, be helped or facilitated to find levels of truth in relation to their life experiences? It may be that most expressions of wandering are in fact forms of seeking. Reading Coelho's and other works, talking to friends or joining a group, are ways to find help for the journey. Whatever approach is used, anything that is disclosed as important in a person's life, has the potential to lead to some meaning, or truth forming, for his or her life. At the same time, it needs to be said that any meaning or truth about life as a whole – worth its salt – has to take into account the heights and depths of human experience, the exhilaration of hill-top visions and of the grimness of darkened valleys. It is especially the case that meaning has to give an account of dark experiences. For Coehlo, it was in his visit to the concentration camp that he was able to gather up and find resonance with his own suffering; then he set himself in the Christian framework to find meaning and spiritual freedom.

My own work in recent years of leading groups of seekers has been in a manner that is life-centred – calling forth people's genuine concerns in such a way that begins to make sense of their life journeys. At the same time stories of the Christian gospels are used. It has been, I believe, a remarkably valuable means of facilitating seekers. These 'journey' groups focus on Easter as a climax of faith finding and forming as well as of commitment, with adult baptism being at the heart of the celebration.

The model that I and others use is that of the revived and adapted fourth century Catechumenate (literally, 'that which echoes within'), as people hear the story of God at work in human life in the Scriptures. In time they are then able to make a personal decision to take on the Christian way of life.

Christian initiation is therefore the topic of this book. In popular terms initiation is identical with the sacramental act of baptism. But, as we shall see, a richer understanding of initiation, based on the classical approach of the early centuries, is crying out to be heard today. The retrieval of a richer understanding expressed in our culture needs to include the following components:

i. welcoming and engaging seekers for faith forming
ii. regaining a vibrant practice of baptism
iii. facilitating a faith walk that makes Christian witness distinctive in society.

The Roman Catholic scholar Aiden Kavanagh in his book *The Shape of Baptism* presents the classical understanding of initiation in terms of preparation of adults leading to 'the water bath' and then to nurturing them in the Christian community. To those in the churches today who say, 'Surely baptism is a simple event and should not be seen as complex', Kavanagh replies:

Nothing so subtly impedes obtaining an adequate grasp of water baptism itself and of Christian initiation as a whole, as the shrunken proposition that the event in water was all that ever was to it, and that all else constitutes highly problematic additions to this originally simple act ... Baptism has always been a compound act absorbing cultural patterns into itself: it has taken on definite shape in various cultures, shaping those cultures in turn.[3]

What is required for us today in order to enrich our view of baptism is to get beneath the legacy of Christendom and uncover the dynamic categories of initiation that are evident in the fourth century and earlier, into the New Testament period itself. These dynamic categories speak of conversion and changed lives, sacramental significance, renewed faith communities and the emergence of a strong social witness. These composite features of initiation are being uncovered today in churches that are using the kind of adult process that Kavanagh and others write about.

Furthermore, this focus digs down beneath the perennial debates in church synods and assemblies that for decades have wrestled with the issues pertaining to infant baptism. The outcome of these debates has largely been to make adult baptism the norm of the Church's life with infant baptism administered on the basis of that norm. The norm of adult baptism, however, is not often evident: the practice of infant baptism still far outweighs the practice of adult baptism. As the norm, it can only make sense when there is visibly a healthy and vigorous preparation and celebrating of adult baptism within local church life.

Ten years of ministry in an Anglican parish in Melbourne, Australia, using the adult process described in these pages, form the basis of my reflections regarding the journey to faith and commitment in a western context. In addition, conversations with others in Australia, the U.K. and North America, where the process has been used, enriched these reflections.

'The Easter Journey' is the name given to the process by many Australian Anglicans. Different names are used in other churches. In the Roman Catholic Church worldwide it is called the Rite of Christian Initiation of Adults (RCIA). In North America "Catechumunate" is maintained. The process is a revival and adaptation of the model used in the early centuries. As we shall see, the process, by being based on people's concerns as well as a personal way of sharing scripture, is designed not as a course or program but as a journey, framed in stages, in order to get alongside and speak to participants' own life journeys.

Seekers of faith are usually unsure seekers, at least in relation to the institutional church. Peter was such a seeker …

FINDING SPIRITUAL COMMUNITY

After their wedding Peter's wife was more interested in church belonging than he was. Yet as a business man who travelled widely he was keen to find a sense of community in the suburb where they had settled. He realised that the church is one of the

> *few hubs of local community left in urban life so he decided a year after his wife participated in the 'Easter Journey' to give it a try himself.*
>
> *Joining that year's group his declared interests were more humane and communitarian than overtly religious. Being heard for what he had to say and hearing the responses of others he began to form a picture in his mind about the Church as a place for all and began also to experience the group as a microcosm of the Church's welcome and acceptance.*
>
> *The spiritual expressions of the Church as community in terms of prayer and worship slowly started to resonate in his personal being and enrich the sense of community that he held dear. The gospels came alive when he began to gain a sense of Jesus as the instigator of a new, just community. He also wanted to contribute in and through the community. The local church was able to direct and support him to meet that need.*

It was by means of a winding progression that Peter was able to come to faith and commitment. There are many similar stories that can be told of people's faith discovery whereby, in and through the breadth and depth of their own lives, Jesus-focussed awakening takes place – usually with key moments as points of conversion.

The method employed in this process is outlined in chapter five. This book, however, is not about how to use the process. There are manuals and guides for that purpose. Rather the thrust here is to present *a vision of initiation*, accessible to many and varied readers, for the future of the Church in which members are oriented to the vision.

Companioning is an important aspect of the process. Church people function as companions to seekers (inquirers). With seekers being 'on the edge' of church life and joining in a group with church people 'of the centre', significant developments occur in the interaction. An edge-centre dynamic arises whereby participants dialogue, learn and grow together.

The first two sections of the book draw on the inspiration of the initiation process as it has been adapted from the fourth century and traces its recent practice in the Church today.

From observing the edge-centre dynamics of the process involving church people and inquirers in parish settings, particular themes emerge and present themselves as potentially relevant for the future of the Church and its mission. I have found a powerful freshness in the emergence of these themes and how they can develop in local church life. These themes will be explored in the third section. They are oriented largely towards the discoverable depths of spirituality as well as the engagement in faith of the harsh edges of our world. In turn, the emergence of these themes strengthens the sense of importance of the adult initiation process.

As a congregation accompanies new people, awareness of being a community of initiation emerges, a community that becomes more conscious of outreach and witness in its corporate identity (fourth section). The celebrating of Holy Baptism regains its spiritually energetic place, free of the over-laden sentimentality of which we are so accustomed in the practice of many infant baptisms.

In these pages we shall immerse ourselves – pun intended! – in the vision of the adult baptismal journey that facilitates spiritual experience and leads to conversion and deepening faith. This vision embraces participants within a process and becomes an avenue of discovery for them. At its core it is a vision of God, wide and alluring. A sixth century writer refers to it at a time when people were being engrafted into the Church in the same kind of process; he likens it to standing on a seashore:

> *God can be known to us in the same way as a person can see an endless ocean standing on the shore at night with a dimly lit candle … He knows there is an ocean in front of him … huge, and that he cannot see it all at once. The same is true of the knowledge of God.*[4]

1. *Juan Arias*, Paulo Coelho: Confessions of a Pilgrim, p.190.
2 *Arias*. p.ix.
3 *The Shape of Baptism: the Rite of Initiation*, Pueblo, 1974, p.xiii.
4 St Simeon's Oratio 61, cited in K. Leech, *True God, an Exploration in Spiritual Theology*, Sheldon London 1985, p.212.

SECTION I

BY THE WATERS

Engaging the Edge

CHAPTER 1

AWE AROUND THE FONT?

Occasions at the Font

It is Easter morning and it is dawn. After their months of discovery the adult seekers have come to faith and stand at the font with their companions. It has been a journey in which struggle, discovery, courage, letting-go and finding afresh, have all been a part of the months leading to this point. The congregation gathers around them, several of whom they have got to know. On this morning there is undoubtedly awe around the font.

One year, on the Sunday after Easter, in the parish in which I was the vicar, I had agreed to officiate at a mid-day infant baptism for a family returning home briefly from their overseas post. If anywhere in the world was their parish it was here. A request for infant baptism in this kind of circumstances is a common occurrence for most parish clergy. As nominal believers there was the usual awkwardness at the celebration with much pastoral cajoling on my part to get them through the event. With mumbled responses and nervousness ... there was no awe on this occasion. Rather, there was nervousness mixed with a shared feeling of "isn't she cute" in relation to the baby being baptised. What a contrast there was between the celebration of the sacrament on Easter Day and this occasion a week later.

Equally we may say that often occasions of infant baptisms of believing families become times of great joy and increased faith. The celebration of the sacrament in this case has its rightful place and legitimacy. What then can the local church do in terms of creative policies in relation to requests for baptism of nominal believers?

No longer can we simply argue that the sacramental action simply 'does the job'. Questions of whether the culture today can sustain such continuing practices need to be asked. These concerns regarding our cultural setting are discussed in the next chapter.

Moreover, basic questions need to be asked today about local practice of the sacrament. Why does it not tend to be regarded with a similar awe and reverence as many people hold for the eucharist? Do we explore other avenues of welcoming and blessing infants sufficiently?

A comparison with the fourth and fifth centuries can be informative. In some ways these centuries as a period of history are not dissimilar to our own in terms of the place of the Church in society. Then and now, the Church is seen as being on the cusp as the official or established religion. Then, the Church was becoming official and gaining a central place; now, it is loosing that role.

An example of how Christian initiation was viewed in the early period can be seen in the following poem from the fifth century. It reflects a spiritually electric atmosphere in relation to the act of baptism. Note how 'awe is struck' in the description given. The sacrament was celebrated at Easter:

Here is born in Spirit-soaked fertility
a brood destined for another City,
begotten by God's blowing
and borne upon this torrent

by the Church their virgin mother.
Reborn in these depths they reach for heaven's realm,
the born-but-once unknown by felicity.
This spring is life that floods the world
the wounds of Christ its awesome source.
Sinner sink beneath this sacred surf
that swallow age and spits out youth.
Sinner here scour sin away down to innocence,
for they know no enmity who are by
One font, one Spirit, one faith made one.
Sinner shudder not at sin's kind and number,
for those born here are holy.[5]

It is not some whipped-up expression of ritual extravagance that produces the heights of inspiration in this poem. Rather it is the commitment and faith of those being baptised and of the community surrounding them, that gives rise to such depths of understanding and passionate perception. The newly baptised would have been involved in a quite lengthy process of preparation, at least over a year, with their companions. Above all there is the holding of the conviction expressed here that it is God who brings about new birth. We can note the strength of the feminine language and other features as well: the other worldly destiny of the baptised, the Spirit's presence and power, the sense of energetic newness of "the sinner in the surf" … "spits out youth", and of wonder and unity in faith.

In a time of great change regarding the place of the Church in society, then as now, we may ask how the theological commentators of each period view the place of baptism in the life of the Church; what should be its right practice as they perceive it to be? Given the present, on-going crisis regarding initiation in the mainstream western churches, a brief survey of this topic is relevant.

The Church Then: the Fourth and Fifth Centuries

In the fourth century the Christian Church was still in competition with the mystery religions such as those of Mithras and Isis. These religions also had rites of initiation (baths of purification) and were accompanied by fasting. In the face of the power of the other religions the Catechumenate provided a route of re-identification for baptismal candidates. At least a year's preparation of talks, group discussion, prayer and companioning formed the basis of the rites and sacramental act, with the work of the Holy Spirit evident throughout. Nurture followed baptism at Easter.[6] Conversion to Christ involved a deep shift of spiritual identity and belonging.

As Edward Yarnold[7] reveals, the Church at the time thought of baptism as a superior ritual event compared to the practices of the other religions. The sacrament was approached as "an awesome mystery" (Chrysostom), far greater than the power of the surrounding cults.

Two understandings of baptism are relevant to our discussion. One is that before the sacrament was celebrated candidates were to be given to prayer, fasting, exhortation, exorcisms as their sponsors closely attended to them. The rites of stripping, immersing, and anointing are not so much emphasised for ritual significance but are seen as pointing to "freedom from slavery", "a share in the indescribable gift of heaven", "being born again as a completely different person."[8] Usually these meanings of the baptismal act were not spoken of with the candidates until after Easter, that is, until the sacramental event had been experienced.

The other understanding is an awareness that Ambrose wrote about in which he expected the initiates may well have been disappointed at what they saw in terms of the font and baptismal space. "You have come to the baptistry, you see the water, the bishop … If you think, "Is that all?" – indeed it is all. Here there is all innocence, all devotion and sanctification. … You saw what is done, what is unseen is much greater than what is seen."[9] The simplicity of symbol compared frugally with those of the mystery religions, in other words the Church was committed to ensuring that the sign is so expressed that it points to that which it signifies, the liberating grace of God in Christ.

To the question that is often asked: were the rites of Christian initiation modified in this period in imitation of the pagan mysteries? Yarnold comments, "the rites themselves were hardly influenced but the explanation given of them began to emphasise the elements of mystery and fear."[10] In this sense we could say that the sacrament was to a deliberate degree enculturated and at the same time remained faithful to its New Testament roots.

The Church Now: the Twentieth and Twenty-First Centuries

Turning to the present we find theologians of our own time largely critical of currently dominant baptismal practice. I refer here to three post Second World War writers. A kind of casualness (in contrast to "the element mystery and fear") with which the sacrament is administered is picked up by each of them.

Dietrich Bonhoeffer is well-known for his juxtaposition of "costly" and "cheap grace" in relation to baptism and the baptismal calling. He challenges the Church to preach the costly grace:

Cheap grace is the preaching of forgiveness without repentance, baptism without church discipline, communion without confession, grace without discipleship … Costly grace is the treasure hidden in the field.[11]

Fellow Protestant theologian Karl Barth's words on the subject are couched in terms of unready receivers of the sacrament being "a wound in the side of Christ":

Baptism without the willingness and readiness of the baptised is true, effectual and effective baptism, but it is not correct baptism; it is not done in obedience, it is not administered according to proper order and is therefore clouded baptism. It is a wound in the side of Christ and a weakness for the baptised … How long is the church prepared to be guilty of the occasioning of this wounding and weakening through a baptismal practice that is arbitrary and despotic?[12]

In the book quoted, Barth in fact argues for believers' baptism and therefore against infant baptism. He has strong words regarding those times when the sacrament is administered with little preparation for those of older years. The Roman Catholic theologian Hans von Balthasar argues in a like manner:

The baptism of infants is inadequate as a model for the sacramental event. To say entrance into God's Kingdom occurs unconsciously … neither perceiving nor understanding Christ's gesture – is a fact so conspicuously alien to scripture that it must be regarded as an exception. The decision for infant-baptism was perhaps the most portentous decision in the entire history of the Church.[13]

Many readers will think that the latter two thinkers hit a little too hard. Many who minister in the present-day Church find it difficult to refuse infant baptism to nominal adherents. As parents their reasons for making a request are frequently not clear and yet at the same time some vague sense of faith can be detected in them. We live in times that are on the final edge of Christendom and of society's post-Christian, pluralist era, hence the decision to be made in pastoral situations is often not easy. (See a further discussion on this issue in Chapter 16.)

The latter two theologians argue that the practice of the past is fundamentally mistaken. If this is so, yet is unavoidably our present legacy, pastoral practice cannot be 'cleaned up' overnight. In this context the Church largely and understandably resorts to a limited theology of baptism that emphasises community welcome and God's acceptance.

The 'mistake' we find ourselves in has mainly been a consequence of Augustine's teaching. Whilst he, as a bishop in fourth century Carthage, was committed to the preparation and baptism of adults as the norm of initiation for most of his ministry, later he taught the doctrine of original sin: that sin is passed on universally from generation to generation, inherited by each child through conception and birth. The British historian David Wright describes this as "the baptismal revolution." The need for infants to be baptised for the removal of its stain developed and by the early medieval period became central church practice. The process of preparation leading to the sacramental act of baptism, and nurture afterwards, fell away.

Finding a True Vision of Initiation

A truer vision of the nature of baptism in terms of conversion, call to discipleship and church membership hence became clouded. The time has come in our period of history, as Bonhoeffer urges in relation to baptism and baptismal living to proclaim costly grace: *grace* with all its discovery of joy and welcome but also costly in terms of the radical giving of oneself to God in service and prayer. This grace is encountered in the preparation for baptism as well as afterwards, such that new Christians shift in their identity from a primary allegiance to the things of this world to an allegiance to the in-coming Reign of God.

In our own time therefore we are challenged to return to more true vision and practice of the sacrament. Such an endeavour calls into question the priority of its role in dealing with original sin, and indeed many would argue, that the concept of original sin may not be credible in any case. The route of the adult initiation process is fundamentally what makes sense as the 4th-5th century Church exemplified. It puts the sacrament into practice in a way that displays its proper meaning.

To venture down this path in terms of local church priorities is to embark on and encounter the wonder of the initiation way, its discoveries and breakthroughs in fellowship and prayer and, yes indeed, to know awe at the font, culturally dissimilar to the fourth century, but with the same commitment to the process of initiation.

It is not the task of this book to mount a criticism of infant baptism as such. I take the note struck by the authors quoted above as a call in our own time to establish a pathway for adult initiation and with it a pathway of renewal of adults who were baptised at a young age.

In the last section of this book I shall discuss the cultural and contextual issues of the present for the baptising community. The challenge that the thrust of this chapter presents is to take the plunge in our present context of being the Church in society: that is, to adopt the initiation pathway that is central yet presently needs uncovering within the Church's life and tradition. 'Taking the plunge' needs to include an enculturated form of initiation. Just as the Church in 4th-5th centuries embraced mystery and fear (akin to but surpassing the mystery religions) thereby enhancing the meaning of baptism as it was practiced at that time, so in our own time we need to embrace the individual journey dimension of our culture for the purposes of initiation.

Whatever the period of history Christians find themselves in, a passion for the Faith, especially as it is manifested in Holy Baptism, has to be evident. As our generation begins to adopt the initiation journey with the gathering at the font of Holy Baptism being the climax of the journey, we may begin to echo these words of the earlier period:

The eyes of the heart are cleansed, there is healing of the passions and of bodily sickness, and the soul is filled with joy and amazement expressed in tears … A person is totally changed and knows God as he is first known by him … the newly baptised cry we've got eternal life in our hearts.[14]

5 Cited in Kavanagh, p.49, Lateran Baptistry, Rome.

6 The source for this information comes from the catechetical instructions of John Chrysostom at Antioch and Cyril at Jerusalem, fourth century.

7 Yarnold, *The Awe Inspiring Rites of Initiation, Baptismal Homilies of the Fourth Century*, St Paul Publications 1977.

8 Yarnold p.56.

9 Yarnold p.66.

10 Yarnold p.67.

11 Dietirch Bonhoeffer, *The Cost of Discipleship*, p.36.

12 *The Teaching of the Church regarding Baptism*, SCM 1948 p.40.

13 *The Glory of the Lord*, T & T Clark 1982 p.579.

14 Simeon the New Theologian, 5th cent. cited in K. Leech *True God*, p.211.

CHAPTER 2

ANCIENT-FUTURE PATHWAY

Much of the reason for the sacramental awe in the Church of the 4th-5th centuries and earlier was that the newly baptised were learning to be Gospel-centred Christians. They had discovered a communal, religious way different from the official empire religion as well as the mystery religions; a way that was based on the living Christ and his liberating Word. Within the context of the Roman Empire the converts' dying and rising in the Easter baptismal mystery meant that they were being transformed in all dimensions of their lives, including their social witness. By learning Christ's way of valuing each and every human life the egalitarian thrust of the Church's life meant that they joined the army of believers who stood against the evils of the empire. However, with the Constantinian establishment of Christianity as the religion of the empire, a softening of both preparation for baptism and social stand, took place during the centuries that followed.

Two contemporary writers trace the significant characteristics of the third to fifth centuries and its relevance for our present time. They hold up helpful insights with regard to opening the treasures of Christianity to church and seeker today. This focus could be called an ancient-future pathway. Both writers are concerned to find illumination from the Church's course in the early period for our own time. They both see a hurdle that needs to be acknowledged and jumped over. The hurdle is the legacy of Christendom that over the centuries has had the effect of overly compromising the gospel message.

The first writer is Alan Kreider in his book, *The Change of Conversion and the Origin of Christendom*. Kreider bases his historical exploration on these claims:

i. Conversion in the early centuries involved not just changes in belief but in behaviour and belonging: the task of conversion was to reshape the person into an entirely new way of living and into a new system of values.

ii. The malaise of western Christianity has to come to terms with the yoke of Christendom in which church and state, church and society have been bound together; this yoke has lessened and compromised the earlier gospel witness.

The other writer is Stanley Hauerwas and his work with William Willimon, *Resident Aliens*, a term used to describe the identity of Christians in the third century, the pre-establishment period of the Church. His approach is as follows:

i. With the establishment of Church within the Roman Empire under Constantine the premise was that the Church shares power within the context of the State without the Church being a problem to the powerful.

ii. The decline of Christendom gives the joyous opportunity to sever this root and to reclaim the freedom to proclaim the Gospel.

If there is a strong measure of truth in these contentions then they are pertinent to any discussion of adult conversion and formation in our own time. Let us therefore look further at what is at stake in these claims.

Changed Lives

A sketch of one of the recorded personal conversions in the early period pictures the radical shift in values that becoming a Christian involved. Cyprian's movement into Christianity in the third century is illustrative of the kind of transformation that occurred for inquirers at the time.

He had been a wealthy man and was well-known for his skill of rhetoric. His preparation and formation brought him to realise "the gilded torments" and "smiling wickedness" of his earlier life. He came to realise that the power of possessions was such that "it possesses their possessor". He encountered the Christian community as a community of thrift in which among other traits plain clothing was the norm. Through the waters of the font what before seemed difficult in terms of change in lifestyle began to appear possible: he became "a free man" having shed his clinging to wealth. When he was accelerated into episcopal leadership he lived simply and opened his home to the poor until he was executed in 258.[15]

During this time of the Church's witness many of the uneducated warmed to the Faith. Congregations became known for their attractiveness and the confidence with which they held their Christian convictions. Religion had customarily a servile, submissive role in the Empire. But with the growth of Christianity "an unprecedented querying of the conventional relationship between religion and the national state and ethnic identity" was clearly evident.[16]

Martyrdom became a characteristic of the pre-Constantinian period. "The blood of the martyrs is the seed of the Church" became an adage of the time. Condemnation to death was not only due to a refusal to take the oath to the emperor or to serve as a soldier but under certain emperors simply being a Christian was sufficient grounds for the shedding of blood. Yet, rather than diminishing the witnessing life of the Church martyrdom strengthened it.

It was the shared life of the Christian community in the early centuries that bred a hostility among those who were in power in the empire. The Epistle of Diognetus written in the second century explores the difference that the Christians displayed:

Inhabiting Greek as well as barbarian cities ... and following the customs of the natives in respect of clothing, food and the rest of their ordinary conduct, they display to us their wonderful and confessedly striking way of life ... They dwell in their own countries but simply as sojourners. As citizens, they share in all things with others, and yet endure all things as if foreigners.[17]

Later in the fourth century, Bishop John Chrysostom (literally "golden mouth", due to his eloquent preaching) at Antioch was a fervent exponent of the vision of conversion. He taught that entering the life of faith purified, ushered the believer into miraculous powers. John exposed the catechumens to extensive hearing of scripture, and through "catechism and awesome rite to enter a new world of solidarity and transformed behaviour."[18]

Compromised Gospel

Decades after Christianity became the established religion distinctive Christian social witness began to decline. The fire of the Gospel became domesticated. No longer were believers encouraged to critique society from the stand point of the Faith. The requisite components of preparation for baptism became limited to doing good works and the necessity of almsgiving, along with ascribing to right belief.

In tracking the relevance of this period to our own, Hauerwas quotes Barth's definition of the Church:

The Church exists ... to set up in the world a new sign which is radically dissimilar to the world's manner and contradicts it in a way which is full of promise.

Hauerwas sees that deliberate and sharpened attention is required to see the Church as having a clear identity distinct from the society in which it is placed. The Church of the early centuries was forming Christians in the alternative story to the world's; this alternative story is God's story with humanity, especially beginning with stories about Jesus:

As Hauerwas puts it:

In relation to fear, confusion and paralysis pervading the society God says 'I brought you out of Egypt, have no idols, journey on with me' ... resulting in communities of resistance to injustice and in there being racial harmony within the Christian assemblies.[19]

The Sermon on the Mount expresses much of true Christian formation in terms of:

forgiveness,
peace-making,
purity of heart,
trusting prayer,
love of enemies,
committed personal and
communal relationships of mutual respect.

Hauerwas sees these patterns as already established by Christ. It is "the inaugural manifesto of how the world looks now that God in Christ takes matters in hand." Essential to this is the invitation not to be other-worldly but to engage and be in the world. He continues:

The Sermon begins with not saying what to do but how to see and cease from seeing the world as permanent; Christians are free to work in a non-violent way. They are free to work in a non-violent way because they know about the End.[20]

This End-time thinking that allows for a strong form of Christian freedom was not to last. Hauerwas comments that the removal of End-time oriented thinking (eschatology) that began in the fifth century led to "the suffocating moralism of the Church."

Turning to the plight of the Church in the present he points to the great opportunity to return to more authentic witness: "salvation is adventure". He argues in addition that we are at the end of the era of the western social experiment (inaugurated by the seventeenth century Enlightenment) with its focus on the individual as free, rational agent. We are increasingly aware of inner and outer forces in the face of which we need to find a way beyond this time of experiment, a way of salvation.

In reviewing the contribution of these authors to identifying the situation of the Church and its future outreach, Kreider delineates what he sees as the key characteristics of Christendom as it became established in European society around the time of the sixth century until the twentieth century. The characteristics fall into three areas:[21]

COMMON BELIEF: ORTHODOX CHRISTIANITY: heresy is not tolerated, unofficial alternatives however live on, religious instruction is often rudimentary, society's symbols, art and ritual are Christian.

COMMON BELONGING: recruitment (christening of all infants), the church and large constituent parishes, church/state symbiosis, lack of choice, clericalism, mission is 'beyond', to remote countries.

COMMON BEHAVIOUR: expectation to behave 'like a Christian', enforcement of behavioural norms, exceptionally committed Christian practice is considered not normal.

Emerging out of these historical shadows is not an easy task, as Kreider points out. A dominant form of religion is uncovered in these expressed characteristics. They stand in contrast to the freedom and to a larger extent the power of the Faith, spiritually and not humanly based, of the earlier period. Kreider, however, acknowledges the great achievement of Christian artists and intellectuals throughout the Christendom period.

Reclaiming the Whole Gospel

The early centuries of the Church's life appear as a "disturbing strangeness" (Brown) and at the same time they are the source of "relevant clues" (Butterworth) for Christians in the post-Christendom era.[22]

As I have already indicated, the process of evangelisation and formation of new Christians that developed in the fourth century became known as the Catechumenate. Adopting and adapting the process in our own time is a way forward through the difficult terrain of becoming a post-Christendom Church in which faithfulness to the Gospel in all aspects of life may be recognised and lived out. The process of its nature is 'edge oriented'. When and if the Church adopts such a process and becomes committed to it, a way then is found gradually to evolve a witnessed lifestyle. The shape of the Christian life is therefore discoverable more by means of a dynamic on the edge than through solely centre-type leadership.

At the same time there are the prophets of our own time who point the way forward for the future character of the Church. Dietrich Bonhoeffer continues to stand out as a prophet of the Christian community in the evolution of its witness. As well as writing extensively about Christian witness before and during the Second World War he also lived for some time in a community of formation and mutual discovery that is not dissimilar to the edge-centre dynamic of the adult Initiation process.

Within the context of the Nazi totalitarian state Bonhoeffer committed himself to the establishment of the seminary at Finkenwalde in southern Germany. It provided a lived communal experience centred on the shared reading of scripture.

Some years before, Karl Barth was instrumental in establishing the Barmen Declaration of the Confessing Church, the essential stance of which was to say that there is only "*ein Fuehrer, Jesus Christ*". In their communal life Bonhoeffer, his colleagues and students were in fact returning to identifying the Church as fundamentally defined by Christ, the Word and not conditioned by society – a church that called people to conversion, that functioned as "a new sign", the visible church engaged in the world and also distinct from it, the church of the cross.

As we shall see in the next chapter, the present-day expression of the Catechumenate is oriented to individual journeyers or seekers. People are accompanied such that contemporary-styled individualism can be transformed into communal belonging and commitment through shared faith encounter: individuality begins to find its true form as being in relationship to others and to God in a shared witness to the New World inaugurated by Jesus.

15 Cited in Kreider p.8.
16 Kreider p.77.
17 Cited in Timothy Radcliffe, *What is the Point of Being a Christian?*, Burns & Oats, 2005, pp.2-3.
18 Kreider p.52.
19 Stanley Hauerwas and William Willimon, *Resident Aliens*, Abingdon Press Nashville 1089, p.52.
20 Hauerwas and Willimon p.87.
21 Kreider p.91 ff.
22 Kreider p.100.

CHAPTER 3

SEARCHERS WELCOMED TO A PROCESS

Seeker and Church

Big issues confront the Church in relation to authentic witness today and in the future. In the midst of this challenge sit the many struggling congregations of our cities, towns and countryside. Some dwindling congregations may continue to complain: "Why don't more people come to our church?". At the same time many congregations are committing themselves to varied and imaginative avenues of outreach and social concern, thus meeting people at their points of need.

The initiation way builds on these avenues of outreach. Outreach creates the opportunity to invite adults into faith exploration and of becoming formed into the Christian life.

The error in much local mission thinking is to think that community family support programs, outreach prayer and praise, packaged introductions to Christian faith, and so on – are all that is required in the making of new Christians and in developing church belonging. As we look at the present and future climate of the Church in society it is clear that without the initiation way these activities stand as incomplete. What is required is the facilitating of faith exploration and forming that builds on these activities.

Quick and easy routes into church belonging and membership often eventuate in a cheapened experience of an introduction to Christianity and also carry the danger that the new-comer's adherence may be temporary or remain superficial. It is 'into the whole gospel' that the Church must ascribe to seekers the dignity of their potential calling and not short-change them with versions of reductionist Christianity. Furthermore, engaging in the practice of the initiation process, the congregation finds itself deepening and broadening its own prayer and mission.

Many a young seeker, tentative or otherwise, has bravely ventured into the ecclesiastical space of the Sunday morning service. I vividly remember a young relative of mine turning up for the Palm Sunday liturgy at which I was presiding. She arrived at the same time as the palm procession entered the church. I knew that she had had very little exposure to the Church and had little knowledge of the Faith. She therefore did not know what all the 'carry-on' was about! She may have comprehended some aspects of what was happening, such as parts of the long Passion reading. I found myself guessing what was going through her mind, but with the service in full swing I could do little to support her apart from providing an occasional, publicly rendered explanatory point. Clearly, by the time the service had progressed to the distribution of communion she was sufficiently mystified to see the need to leave. Her departure came as no surprise to me.

Many will comment on this incident to suggest, "simplify the service" … "make it more accommodating". In recent decades the Church has worked hard to modernise the language and style of liturgy. More may need to be done in some areas, such as in the case of hymns and music, often in bondage to the Victorian era. Basically, however, the view-point that the form of the eucharist is not something to mess around with needs to be emphasised.

In wrestling with this kind of situation a priest colleague once commented, "the mass does not give its secrets away easily." In other words, we have to acknowledge that this centre and heart of Christian community life, this hearing and feeding on Christ, done with order and reverence, is indeed a learned art, an art well worth acquiring, guaranteed as it is, to impart spiritual treasures to participants till their dying days.

In contemporary society those who wish to inquire, who are prepared 'to put a foot inside the door' of the Church, are usually people who know only a little of the Christian tradition. It is in fact advisable to say to them, 'don't come to the Sunday service to start with, but to a group in which your questions and concerns can be put, into which you with others will be able to be introduced to the Jesus of scripture'. This approach, inherent in the adult initiation process, is to welcome inquirers on their own level, offering them the Good News in the accessible terms of its own call and with the invitation to journey into the fullness of life in Christ.

The growing ignorance about the nature of the Christian Faith throughout western society is what some Christian educationalists have been concerned about for some decades. There are consequences for the future of baptism. The Christian educationalist John Westerhoff has brought clarity to this concern by pointing out that present-day western culture cannot sufficiently support the nurture of faith and forming of Christian values that the community and the networks of family, friends and institutions supported in the past.[23] Over the past fifty years there has been a significant decline of numbers of children attending Sunday schools, of religious education in schools, of children having regular contact with Christian friends and members of the wider family, and, of exposure to Christian values in the media and society at large.

The waves of secularism and pluralism define the advent of the post-Christian era. As a consequence the manner in which the Church initiates people in the Faith needs major rethinking. Westerhoff's assertion, picking up Tertullian's adage of the third century, that "Christians are made not born", succinctly sets the agenda for the future Church.

Like Paulo Coehlo, mentioned in the introduction, many people in our modern-day culture see their life journey as primary data, the "caravan" which any truth-telling claim must address. The inductive group approach used in the adult initiation (catechumenal) process allows for the naming and exploration of the height and depth of a person's experience such that in contemplating scripture the Spirit is able to get alongside and speak to that person.

Adult Initiation Process Revival

As a vehicle to aid people into faith and discipleship in our time the Catechumenate re-emerged in the 1950s and '60s in Africa and in France. Adopting the pattern of the fourth century structure there are four stages used in the process, as Chapter 5 describes in more detail. Care was taken in its modern expression to frame the process for a holistic discovery of the Christian faith so that, for example, in the formative period prayer, worship, scripture, sacraments, ministry and solidarity with the poor, each has a place.[24]

In the same manner as the earlier version an emphasis on stages (with rites) and companions was put in place. At the same time two differences with the original approach emerged. The first was an adaptation that is foundational for the modern expression of the Catechumenate, namely, that in having the story of God's dealing with humanity 'echoed' in the lives of the inquirer, the people's stories were deemed significant both for the persons themselves and others. A theological premise undergirds this approach, namely, that God is at work in the human person before he or she comes to faith. This providential care of the divine, Calvin called "prevenient grace". As group participants reflect on their lives the traces of God's grace can be recognised in their past experiences. Of course other parts of a person's life need review and expressions of repentance. Repentance, however, in its fundamental meaning as change of heart and mind becomes the critical step for inquirers within the whole process.

The other difference is in relation to the use of scripture whereby a personal, intuitive approach is adopted in which group members participate.

Overall, the process is an inductive approach that 'goes with the flow' of the group's concerns, yet in stages. It differs from the programmatic courses that aim at presenting the faith to seekers. These courses have their place in the endeavour of outreach as an introduction to the Faith. The 'Easter Journey' however is vital in terms of conversion and forming people.

A couple of objections regarding the fundamentals of the process are often raised at this point. One objection is to do with the place of experience and the other to do with the view that the process may be too difficult in practice. Firstly, then, it is asked, 'does exploring human experience really have a place in coming to faith?' It has already been said that a theological premise is that God is at work in human experience. What can be said further is that in the kind of inductive approach named here the dialogue of scripture and experience in a group context genuinely brings about spiritual awakening and conversion.

The usual approach of the twentieth century in seeking to bring adults to faith has been to *explain* the ways of faith as a didactic approach. Some readers will remember the days of adult confirmation classes when a book was used to present the doctrines of the Church. Somehow this one-sided rationalistic approach was meant to convert, yet it was an appeal to the mind only. Narrowing down the Christian inquiry to 'explaining faith' is in the vein of the Enlightenment whereby reason has been exalted to be the sole judge of what is acceptable or not.

Fortunately, in the Church in the West as well as in developing countries, ways and means that gather up experience are being included in the opening up of the Faith for people.

The missiologist David Bosch writes:

Metaphor, symbol, ritual, sign and myth, long maligned by those interested only in "exact" expressions of rationality are today being rehabilitated; they create forms that synthesize and evoke the integration of mind and will."[25]

It is precisely therefore in the use of an open-ended process that human experience is honoured and scripture accessed in a personal fashion. Participants are helped to find find their way towards "an integration of mind and will" which in Christian terms amounts to a discovery of one's true identity and direction in Christ.

The other objection is that in introducing the adult initiation process to clergy and lay leaders some have said that it appears too hard. The response here is to assure leaders that there is definitely a hardship involved and it is to do with 'going with the flow' of the process, journeying with people and not needing to have all the answers. Once this difference to didactic models is grasped and leaders in their first experience of the process are supported then a way forward is usually found.

Welcoming searchers to the process is best done in stages. As we shall see in more detail there is freedom to leave the process at the end of either the first two stages. In the realities of parish life some people who choose to join a group may not see themselves as searchers or seekers but have got some understanding and acceptance of Christianity. They may have been attending church for some time with a 'half-baked' faith. Others are new to the parish, to church culture, 'off the street', maybe with links into forms of New Age practice and are looking for meaning or for community … In various ways each inquirer is looking for 'the water of life' (the topic of the next chapter).

A Theology of Welcome

The topic of welcoming requires some deliberate attention. What is contained in a theology of welcome? How does Christian welcoming differ from other cultures of welcoming? As I and others have learnt, in attempting to be a part of a welcoming approach to the new-comer in a congregation, it is far more than being simply 'friendly' in the cultural sense that we are familiar with that term.

Australian Uniting Church minister Dr John Brown some years ago wrote a powerful article, Jesus' *New Community at the Periphery*,[26] for the purpose of assisting the debate on sexuality in that church, especially in relation to those who are different.

Brown turns to Luke's Gospel to ask a key question in relation to welcoming: who are the people especially invited into the new community of Jesus?

The first group named as those who are especially invited are the Samaritans – a despised half-breed, even considered enemies of God. In the parable of the Good Samaritan the Samaritan is praised as knowing better than the priest and Levite what love of God and neighbour are. Only a Samaritan returns to give thanks to Jesus of the ten lepers healed. That Jesus offers them full membership of his community is seen in John's Gospel where the woman at the well (Ch. 6), an estranged woman in her own community, comes to draw water in the middle of the day and there is offered salvation, living water.

There is then a second group – the women. Jesus' relationship with women leaves him vulnerable to accusations of impropriety. In the same scene in John 4 the disciples return astonished to see him talking to the Samaritan woman. Again in Luke, Jesus encourages Mary (in the Mary and Martha account of Ch. 10) to become a disciple, despite the Jewish culture of discipling that saw women as not having the intelligence to learn the Law. Jesus' mother in Luke is regarded as the model believer as she proclaims the God who exalts the humble in the song of the Magnificat.

In addition, the faith of foreigners is affirmed, a Roman slave is healed and even tax collectors are accepted – all these are given a special place in Jesus' community of the incoming Reign of God.

The Church therefore is called to live and witness in this way. In every generation there will be the rejected, the outsiders, those discriminated against who in the way of Jesus are to be genuinely welcomed. More than this, in so doing, it is 'on the edge' that the community of Jesus is formed and then finds itself again in order to re-form.

Welcoming therefore involves a spiritual-social understanding of 'the other', that sees him or her as one who is potentially marginalised and yet important to God's purpose. The gates must be flung wide open. We can see that the true pulse or rhythm of Christ's community is where grace is continually encountered on the edge: it is here that we acknowledge and embrace vulnerability, here that the Spirit works and heals foremost. For inquirers it is here that the search for truth, together with companions, becomes fertile as 'centre' and 'edge' open up to each other, that life stories can be told so that Christ's healing of suffering can be known and the paths of God can be found together.

Lord our God. who anointed your only Son
with the Spirit at the river Jordan,
and so hallowed the waters of new birth
to bring us forth to salvation:
keep us strong in life and grace,
direct the ways of your people
and open the door of your kingdom
to all who stand upon the threshold of faith …
(Society of St Francis Celebrating Common Prayer, p.114)

23 *Will Our Children Have Faith?*, Morehouse Publishing 2000 p.10 f.

24 The revival of the Catechumenate in the Roman Catholic Church was formalised as a result of the Second Vatican Council. In parallel to the role of the Rite of Christian Initiation of Adults (RCIA) in the Catholic Church the Anglican and Lutheran Churches, as well as some of the Reformed Churches, have developed the process in similar ways but with slight variations of detail.

25 D Bosch, *Transforming Mission*, Orbis 2004 p.353. In this quote Bosch continues: "So we see an upsurge of interest, especially in third-world churches, in narrative theology, theology as story and other non-conceptual forms of theologising." He does not suggest an abandoning of rationality but its expansion.

26 *Sexuality, Exploring the Issues*, Joint Board of Christian Education, 1996.

CHAPTER 4

WATER: SYMBOL OF LIFE

How dramatically the Christian scriptures portray water in life! There is the wonder of water, drawn from a well, still and pure, as a thirsty Jewish man Jesus, against custom, asks a foreign woman for a drink. He ends up offering her "living water" so that she will "never thirst again." Just as in the Australian outback with its unrelenting heat a lost traveller will cry out in dire thirst for water, we all thirst for the pure fresh springs of the water that is new life, offered according to the gospels by Jesus.

As we shall see in this chapter the use of the sign of water in Holy Baptism is essentially a grace-laden sign when as an event it is prepared for through the journey of gathering up personal experiences and coming to know Christ. An exploration of the meaning of water reveals the appropriateness of the symbol as it is used in the sacramental act and enriches our understanding of what is happening in the lead-up to, within and reflecting upon the sacred event.

Contrasting Meanings

The Israel of the Old Testament was a dry land. The refreshment and even the salvation that God brings is often likened to a spring in the desert. "I will give you water in the wilderness, a river in the desert (Isa.43:19), and, "The Lord God is my strength and my song ... With joy you will draw water from the wells of salvation" (Isa. 12:2-3).

The spring in its purity and loveliness reminds us of original innocence. Mountain bush walking is a favourite past-time of mine. There is little more that depicts innocence than to sit quietly by a mountain spring. To sit there is to get in touch with the innocence of our birth and hopefully the intimations of new and eternal life that grace gives.

Thinking of this innocence today leads to the awareness of what happens to water in the hands of humanity: we are reminded of our fallenness and the need for fresh springs to save us from our greed and misuse of creation: I wrote the following poem during a brief rest by a spring whilst on a bushwalk in the Australian alps:

MOUNTAIN SPRING

Source of life, delighting beauty
Where will your end be?
Joyous purity, lovely wonder
Does your innocence with us stay?

I cannot touch fear
As I sit in your company
Rippling, sunlit glistening
Assurance of constant flow

Back of mind knows the prospects
Of your future in the human hand:
Down the slopes, through the valleys
Awesome, downwards to danger and decay

Plummeting, pounding
Into streams of doubtful promise
Expanding, engulfing

Into the great rivers of man

Wars are muted over your
Scarcity, waste and want
Brothers, sisters, where shall we turn
To ensure the purity we spy?

Days later, in the city, I think back –
that spring is still – always – flowing.

Although humans misuse water, it nevertheless powerfully represents a gift of purity and refreshment, cleansing and renewal, innocence and growth. Scripture speaks of water in this way.

At the same time there is a contrasting theme in the scriptures that speaks of water in life as a chaotic force. We are familiar with this very different meaning of water as it presents itself in nature, in the frequent occurrences of disasters such as floods and tidal waves. Anyone who has had the misfortune to nearly drown or see another person drown in the wild surge of the ocean or the dark depth of a river knows about the destructive force of water in its chaotic aspect.

Based on these observations of how water functions in nature we can say that in terms of being an image of life it carries a composite image of contrary meanings – of refreshment, renewal and restoration to life, and, of destructive forces.

Water as Chaos

The theme of water as representing chaos has a long trajectory within the Scriptures.[27] In the book of Genesis God does not create out of nothing but out of chaos, the chaos represented by waters and darkness that produce terror and despair. In the cosmology of the writer God subdues the waters of chaos establishing dry land for things to grow, relegating the waters to the boundaries.[28] God holds back the destructive forces for life to emerge and be sustained. Life is pictured in a form of innocence. This is the creative act of God.

Then, developments involving water take place as the biblical drama unfolds. Due to human greed God cannot hold back the forces of chaos. God gathers a few people for them to survive the ensuing flood. Entering the ark entails the establishing of a covenant relationship between humanity and God, a covenant of universal respect for life and God's promise of providential care.

As Israel's history continues there is an equally dramatic passage through the waters of chaos into a new dimension of life and living. From the despair and helplessness of slavery in Egypt the people pass through the Red Sea led by God – as on dry land – with the Egyptian pursuers becoming overwhelmed by the winds whipping up chaotic waters. Out of this chaos God calls a new community, a rebuilt nation which is entered into through another crossing – through the Jordan River that constitutes the boundary of the promised land.

Through the ages Israel baptised converts from other nations and in so doing recapitulated its sacred history in that person. Being immersed bodily in the waters symbolises passage through the primeval chaos, the flood-time wickedness of the people, the bondage in Egypt and crossing Jordan River into the land of promise. The emergence from the waters initiates the person into the nation and its call by God.

Centuries later John preaches repentance by the Jordan. Jesus comes and is baptised "to fulfil all of God's demands" (Matt.3). He is to lead a new passage out of the waters of chaos *by* going all the way down into the watery chaos himself. Mark describes Jesus' baptism as *into (eis)* the waters. By virtue of John's baptism Jesus takes up Israel's history as his own and commits himself to the further, final crossing into the effective Reign of God, a crossing which he will undertake through the baptism of his death.

In Orthodox iconography of the Baptism of Christ, Jesus is depicted as naked or near-naked as he stands enveloped in the water of the Jordan. The water is dark or black indicating the path to death that he in obedience must take.

In the New Testament the apostolic community makes it clear that entrance into the community is by baptism into the death and resurrection of Jesus. Those who did not live through these events as they happened in history are to recapitulate them in a celebration of the community as rebirth from despair to hope, from defeat to the explosion of new possibilities of life (1Peter 3 & Rom. 6). Paul preaches the notion of "a newness" in terms of all the baptised sharing in the common destiny of God's Reign – full cleansing and entry into God's new community (letter to the Hebrews) and no more discrimination between races, sexes or classes of people (Gal. 3).

Hence, in this salvation history, at various stages of God's dealing with the people, God redeems them from the destructive powers of the 'waters of chaos' until the point when something categorically different and final happens in and through Jesus. His immersion into the watery chaos enacted in the Jordan is to bring healing to life *within* the course of this world, to restore all life, to overcome the cost of one group expended at the price of another's freedom: this fullness of life restored is achieved in the mission of Jesus. His followers must therefore enter this path. The water bath symbolises entry into Christ's dying and rising life in the power of the Holy Spirit – to lose one's life in order to gain it, to resist evil in the world by faith and hence to know the victory of Christ in one's inner being.

The Waters of Baptism

Immersion in water or the pouring of water in the service of baptism is, as the Jewish rite before it, a recapitulation of God's saving acts of the past, especially the baptism and death of Jesus. With Jesus Christ at the centre of this recapitulation the sacrament act is salvific (or saving): the newly baptised is drawn into Christ and his pattern of life. Alexander Schmemann, an Eastern Orthodox theologian, goes as far as to say:

Creation, fall and redemption, life and death, resurrection and life eternal … the entire content of the Christian faith are held together in their interdependence and unity in this one symbol – of water at baptism.[29]

Let us return to the other side of the image of water, namely, as a gift of renewal, innocence and purity. To be given the water that wells up to eternal life is the gift of Christ to all people, no matter how unworthy they themselves or others deem them. The invitation to "come to the waters" then is an invitation to come to refreshment and renewal as well as a deliberate, committed intention to strive with Christ against all that is chaotically wrong within and without.

Such are the meanings of the symbol of water as pertain to Holy Baptism. The pathway of initiation climaxes in water baptism, to descend and arise with Christ to new life. The powerful symbolism of the event makes little sense without the pathway of preparation to the water bath and nurture, as new born, afterwards. The meanings of water both as a created element and as 'a key player' in the biblical drama of redemption, alert us to the significance of the Initiation way, with immersion in water placed at the centre of the process.

Finally, observing nature can often evoke a deepening of the sense the mystery of baptism and of the call to a wonder-filled life in Christ. One day when returning to Melbourne where I live I found myself amongst the beautiful tall eucalyptus that grow in forests to the east of the city. Their Latin name is *Regnans*. I composed these lines as I pondered their grandeur amidst a dull, rainy day:

REGNANS

Trunks so slender and grand
On slopes so steep, I stop and see
Seemingly defying nature's norm
Many, amassed, spread and sprawling
Swaying as with grace abounding
Glistening with growth
From spring showers.

Through all seasons surely summoning
Possibilities and purpose to pursue
Habitat of hope and even healing
Towards heaven's home.

Seeded yet soaring
Interred yet towering
Beneath – moist, mulched, musty
Succulent subterranean
Where worms and wombat weave and wander
Humus of new beginnings
As of baptism's birthing, bubbling, bursting, bloody,
beckoning.

Crowned with wet weather's dew
So too the clue, the cross of life on forehead creased
To feel and know before, above, beside
And beneath fresh fellowship and fight fermenting.

Edge of city sighted to inspire
Pilgrims passing these knighted nobles
So from font forward
To follow One founded

In our furrows – who reigns
Urging us to rise and revel in
Grace and glory gifted, given.

Likewise, the following prayer uses the image of water to give expression to the graceful character of being a baptised person:

Blessed are you Lord our God, redeemer and king of all;
from the waters of chaos you drew forth the world
and in your great love fashioned us in your image.
Now, through the deep waters of death
You brought your people to new birth
by raising your Son to life in triumph.
May we, the first fruits of your new creation
rejoice in this new day you have made;
may Christ your light ever dawn in our hearts
as we offer you our sacrifice of thanks and praise.
(Anglican Society of St Francis Celebrating Common Prayer, p.13.)

27 I am indebted here to the work of Monika Hellwig, *The Meaning of Baptism*, Plaum/Standard 1972, in her chapter Baptism and community commitment.

28 "G von Rad in his book *Genesis* speaks of chaos as "reality that once existed in a pre-primeval period but also … is a possibility that always exists. Man has always suspected that behind all creation lies the abyss of the formlessness; that all creation is ready to sink into the abyss of the formless; that the chaos therefore signifies the threat to everything created." (p.48 f.)

29 *Of Water and the Spirit*, St Vladimir's Press 1995 p.40.

SECTION II

IMMERSION

Finding Faith on the Edge

CHAPTER 5

THE 'EASTER JOURNEY'

At this point a description of the 'Easter Journey' process will be helpful. Aspects of the process have been mentioned thus far but here I shall outline the process systematically.

Called by its traditional title in some quarters, the Catechumenate as a process proceeds in stages. People inquiring into the Christian faith embark on a group journey. The learning process emphasises an inter-active approach. It becomes a dialogue between people's stories and 'the God Story' and includes a particular response form of reading scripture together. It is a process of coming to conversion and of personal healing.

The process is a baptismal Easter journey. Participants are involved in a double movement that is towards commitment at the Easter font and at the same time a dying to 'the old' to rise to 'the new' as they find their life in Christ. Baptism and/or Confirmation or Re-affirmation of Faith take place on Easter Day or during the Easter Season.

The congregation is a vital part of the process. Congregational members take on the role of being sponsors/companions in the group. Some members may decide in any one year to join the group and to take the journey of Re-affirmation of Faith. Furthermore, the whole congregation has an important role of creating a welcoming environment as the group participants begin to attend the Sunday service.

What's in a name? The word Cathecumenate derives from the foundational period of its use in the 4th to 6th centuries. It refers to a 'the process of instructing (catechesis) or 'of hearing'. Many parishes today do not use the title due to the awkwardness of the word. "The Easter Journey" is the favoured title of many parishes and is the preferred name of the process in this book. Included among alternatives are "the Faith Seeking Journey" and "Becoming Disciples".

The aim of the process is for seekers to come to personal faith and commitment proceeding by way of their questions and concerns, sharing stories of faith and of scriptural encounter. The Catechumenal or 'Easter Journey' way does not use a didactic, programmatic approach. Rather, it goes 'with the flow' of the group and at the same time is bounded in stages. As participants find faith and grow in faith they begin to discover their own ministries and see themselves of members of the Church. This 'way' therefore involves entering Christian community, becoming oriented to prayer, ministry, outreach and justice, in a shared life.

As a parish undertakes this form of local evangelism and nurturing of faith the congregation becomes challenged by the presence of those who are doing and have done the 'Easter Journey'. Changes usually begin to occur in the parish culture.

The Stages

<u>1. Preparing a Catechumenal Team</u>

With the support of others in the diocese or wider church the parish priest/minister brings together a small group from within the parish to be trained as leaders with the clergy. The team meets regularly throughout the process between group sessions.

2. Gathering

Weeks before the first group meeting the congregation is asked to invite people they know to join. An information pamphlet is prepared. Some in the congregation are gatherers in a special way having the gift and keenness of inviting and encouraging others to become inquirers.

REFLECTION STAGE Time of reflection → Ministry	PENTECOST
BAPTISM/CONFIRMATION / REAFFIRMATION RITE	EASTER (March/April)
CANDIDACY STAGE Time of final preparation	LENT (Febrauary/March)
CALLING RITE	ASH WEDNESDAY
FORMATION STAGE Time of learning and growing	December to Febraury
WELCOME RITE	ALL SAINTS DAY
INQUIRY STAGE Time of inquiry	August to November

3. Inquiry

In August/September inquirers come together with some of the congregation who will become sponsors. The first introductory meeting could be a meal. During Inquiry hopes and expectations are shared, questions and concerns are raised and explored.

Inquirers are introduced to the three-fold aspects of the process in terms of 'story' – each others' stories, 'God's story' (of the Bible) and the Church's story (local and wider). Any persons who wish to be confirmed or re-affirm their faith are welcome to join the process.

The number of pre-arranged sessions of Inquiry can range from five to ten in number – usually 1 1/2 hours in length – after which inquirers choose to move into the next phase or not. For those who choose not to continue there may be an alternative group available.

4. Formation

This phase begins usually on Advent Sunday with participants being welcomed at a Sunday service during which they are asked publicly if they wish to continue to explore the Christian Faith. They are also asked the classic catechumenal question belonging to this point of the process, "What do you seek?", to which the invited response is, "Life in Christ" – a response which is unpacked as sessions proceed. Participants are urged now to attend church each Sunday. The congregation is requested to pray for and support them. Each person is given a bible.

Companions (sponsors) are assigned to candidates (as inquirers are traditionally called from this stage on). Each pair of companion and candidate is encouraged to meet together between sessions. Group sessions include scriptural sharing in the intuitive response manner of the African Bible Study method (see box at the end of the chapter) and telling more of life stories, often using a "life map" exercise. Further questions and concerns are explored leading to a focus on the life of prayer and discussing central Christian themes such as the cross and resurrection, the bible, the eucharist, caring service and justice. Regular discussion is also devoted to "what is it like for you attending church?".

The style of proceeding is formational in the sense of assisting candidates to come to faith in a way connected to their lives and to help each other in this endeavour as they discover together. Team leaders at times present issues or topics. Occasionally a handout on a topic may be helpful. Discussion is oriented towards being a person of prayer, discerning ministry and service in the community and wider world.

5. Intense Formation (Candidacy)

This phase begins on Ash Wednesday with weekly meetings throughout Lent, again commencing with a rite in the Sunday service or Ash Wednesday in which candidates express their intention to proceed to Baptism, Confirmation or Re-affirmation of Faith.

In the sessions issues of commitment, baptism, prayer and core aspects of the Faith are further discussed as needed. The promises of baptism are carefully considered. One or two further rites on Sundays may take place (giving of the Lord's Prayer, Creed) as helpful symbols and connection points with the congregation. A retreat may take place in the Lenten period. In churches of the episcopal tradition the "rite of election" can be celebrated with the diocesan bishop in the local cathedral on the fifth Sunday of Lent.

6. Easter

The parish priest/minister has an interview with each candidate before Easter (and possibly at the end of other stages as well). Sometimes the bishop or a visiting minister may spend some time with the candidates. Baptism, Confirmation and Re-affirmation of Faith are celebrated, depending on the denominational tradition, with the bishop or minister presiding, taking place on Easter Day or in the Easter season.

7. Reflection (traditional name: Mystagogy)

Some sessions after Easter are held to share the experience of Easter, to deepen the understanding of the sacraments, to draw out each other's gifts and to explore how participants can move into forms of ministry in the parish and strengthen their ministries in their families, at work and beyond. Group closure is usually the final focus with a commissioning at Pentecost sometimes being held. Bringing the process to closure is sometimes a difficulty for group members as they have developed strongly supportive relationships with each other. Some continued form of group life therefore can often be seen as advisable with possibly some others from the parish joining the group.

The stages as they are described here follow quite closely the description in most manuals used by practitioners (see the end of the chapter for more details regarding resources).

Note on terminology:

> Various names traditionally have been given to participants in the Catechumenal process according to the stages:
> "inquirers" during the Inquiry stage;
> "candidates" during the two stages till Easter
> "graduates" after Easter.
> "Catechumens" refers to those preparing for baptism and possibly Confirmation. Some people find these appellations too formal or stilted, often replacing them with more general words like "participants" or "'Journey members"; these latter terms normally include reference to the sponsors. Likewise the word "companions" has been found more user-friendly than "sponsors". Furthermore, the titles ascribed to the stages sometimes comes under review. For example, Formation and Intense Formation have been designated the Discipleship stage and a suggestion for the Reflection is the Apostolate stage.

Distinctiveness of the Process

The distinctiveness that the Catechumenate as an outreach model can be summed up in its being based upon the Great Commission (Matt. 28:19-20):

> *Go and make disciples of all nations, baptising them in the name of the Father, the Son and the Holy Spirit, and teaching them to obey all that I have commanded you. And remember I am with you always, to the close of the age.*

The elements of "go", "make disciples", "baptise", "teach" and "remember" are all included in this model. "Go-ing" takes place in engaging those on the edge; "teach-ing" occurs especially by way of the group turning to the Word in scripture; "making disciples" emerges as participants are formed, and, at appropriate moments the presence of Christ is named and "remembered" in the group. Then there are some who offer themselves to be "baptised".

The following points describe this distinctiveness in more detail:

i. Process not Program

Making disciples (v.19) today needs to be an inter-active endeavour whereby seekers, their views and experiences, are taken seriously and responded to. This means that the group must proceed according to where its members 'are at', yet within a framework (the formatted stages) which ensures that the process is moving towards its goal. A curriculum-styled program, even with alternatives, does not provide a sufficiently open approach. The 'Easter Journey' is broadly structured and at the same time is open-ended to a significant degree so that themes can be pursued according to need. A private journal that is provided assists participants in helping them keep track of what is important to them and provides a facility to express any thoughts and feelings.

ii. Use of Scripture

The African Bible Study Method that was developed in Africa in the 1960s is the model used in the process. It is an intuitive approach. Sometimes it is called "Gospel Encounter" since the passages most often used are gospel stories (the Gospel reading of the coming Sunday or other suitable passages). The emphasis of the approach to scripture here is that it requires a personal response of group members.

What is foremost in making disciples is the dialogue between the participants and the Word as it comes to them in the context of community and in particular in the group setting. In this use of scripture there is a recovery of bible story to do its work as story, allowing it to touch the hearer. Even for doubting seekers their responses are to be honoured and echoed back to them as they ponder and work with aspects of the Word addressing them. The scriptural passages, according to this listening method, soon are seen as holy ground as text interacts with the realities of each person's life, doing so differently and yet in a mutually helpful manner for each person. The presence or activity of the Other, of God-for-us, of the Spirit, is detected and named either at the time or (more often) in reflection some weeks later.

As group members see the disciples of Jesus reacting and responding to him so they begin to see that they also can become disciples, 'warts and all'. This manner of engaging scripture is in community, that is, Jesus' message is mediated through the group as members listen together. A current of learning flows in accordance with a sense of participating in the teaching of "all that I commanded you."

iii. Baptismal Centrality

"And baptise them in the name …" (v.19). Baptism is central to the practice of evangelism. It is the pinnacle. Baptism is entry in the community of faith, the Body of Christ. The necessary link between being on the edge of the Church with non-believers who are prepared to engage in faith-oriented conversation that is not superficially churchy, and, engrafting them into church life and belonging, is maintained in the process. The sacrament of baptism serves as the focus of this link. Jesus gives the Great Commission immediately after his death and resurrection. The Easter sacramental event of baptism becomes in the process the climax of the participants' journey. The process is baptismal in that:

i. they experience the 'turn-around' of changing their minds (repentance)
ii. they are moving towards commitment to follow the risen Jesus; and,
iii. they are experiencing the giving up of old, wasteful ways of life to embrace the new ways God's grace provides, in order to walk in newness of life.

<u>iv. Edge-Centre Dynamic</u>

There is a distinctive dynamic that evolves from individuals outside the Church or on its edge meeting together with church members. Those 'of the centre' of the Church's life during the process gain or regain the sense of a world-connected faith which church attendance alone in the long-term has difficulty in providing. The church community can become more real and related to daily need, pressures and joys.

<u>v. On a Journey with Stories</u>

In moving away from a syllabus-laden curriculum to a shared journey, attention is given to the questions and concerns people bring. The group leadership facilitates listening to enable openness to each other and to God's Spirit. The journey approach is about sharing life stories; it is about choices (which way to go) according to the challenges God puts in the path. It is also about acknowledging that on the one hand there are frequently no easy answers and on the other that there are discoveries to be made, joys and excitement to be encountered as people fall in love with Jesus and the Kingdom, letting go and letting God …

Group size is an important factor in shared journeying. Eight to twelve is usually regarded as the preferred number, providing enough variety of personalities and enough space for the individual reflection. Larger groups can function, however, dividing into smaller groups for some discussions. Privacy needs to be respected and buffers regarding potential manipulation of others, crying needs of recognition and 'hobby horses' … should be in place.

Group mix is encouraged; homogeneity is not. Basic to the process is the inclusion of young and old, educated and less educated, different races (and even different languages).

Bonding develops and is highly regarded, as inter-personal dynamics aid the emergence of faith and commitment. Conversion takes place gradually and sometimes suddenly with particular moments of profound spiritual encounter. God's forgiveness is experienced sometimes in response to a clear form of repentance, at other times simply as being deeply accepted for oneself.

vi. Marked by Stages and Rites

At the end of both the Inquiry and the Formation period participants are given the option to withdraw from the process. The local church usually will need to have a form of on-going inquiry/exploration available for such people.

As I have indicated above, to mark the transition to the next stage, a small rite is included in the main act of Sunday worship wherein, appropriate to the particular stage, participants are publicly prayed for and are given the opportunity to express their willingness to continue. The companions and congregations are asked to support them by prayer and fellowship.

vii. Addressing the Whole Person

The process continuously requires a response of the heart and not just of the head. As the 'Easter Journey' proceeds, believing with the mind and inviting felt faith is always important. Some leadership teams use art to foster the heart dimension and the way of conversion. Addressing the whole person is to do with heart, mind and body – and relational life in community. Issues of communal belonging and an orientation to practical caring action – all need to be included as a participant approaches Easter.

Using *a journal* from the first meeting on is essential whereby group members are encouraged to write, scrawl, sketch their responses, thoughts, feelings. The use of drawing, of imagination, of music and song, and other techniques that work with the feeling level are often very helpful in gathering up aspects of the whole person into response to God's call.

The 'body' aspect of addressing the whole person is also about 'where we direct our feet', where we go in the community, do we avoid the poor? Opportunities can be provided for an immersion in community service in terms of involvement with vulnerable people in ways not directly experienced before.

viii. Initiated into the Whole Gospel

The process focuses on the Reign of God as Jesus inaugurated it in the Gospel record, facilitating participants into the immersion of prayer, worship, discipleship/ministry and solidarity with the poor. The baptismal language is intentional. Acquiring a sense of belonging to the Church gains depth and breadth. At times in episcopal churches the presence of the bishop is included in the process at one or more points in order to indicate that becoming a part of the Church and its witness is more than a local congregational concern. The bishop represents the unity of the Church at mission in the world.

ix. Cathecetical Evangelism

Kerygma (proclamation) and didache (teaching) combine in the catechumenal process. A gospel story approach in group sessions connects with people at their own level of understanding and need. It functions both as kerygma and didache. In the listening group environment participants hear the Word proclaimed and begin to be taught the way of Christ. The story approach is more engaging and productive than presenting a set of basic beliefs to discuss and debate. Encouragement is given to explore the life and teachings of Jesus. Together with the reflections offered in relation to the questions people ask and the concerns they raise, a dynamic form of catechesis evolves.

x. Communal Ministry

Over a few years of its use many in a congregation will have direct experience of the process as companions, 're-affirmers' or as recently baptised and confirmed. The parish council and the whole congregation are challenged to see its importance as a means of making new Christians. Stimulated by the process people gradually grow in their ministry, of pastoral listening, of articulating their faith, of welcoming, in their understanding of scripture and in outreach (especially of gathering). The congregation then inevitably is challenged to face a deeper review of competing parish priorities.

Some Misunderstandings

The first misunderstanding that arises in learning about the catechumenal process is to do with it being called a "model." The use of the word "model" to describe how the process works in relation to evangelism and formation is used here with hesitation. When first hearing of the process people naturally liken or compare it to evangelistic models used in the Church such as Alpha or Emmaus. These courses often serve a valuable introductory function and can complement the 'Easter Journey'. After gaining some understanding of the process we begin to realise that it is more than a tool or device to be used and is in fact a or the way of 'being church'. Since the Church of its nature is fundamentally initiation focussed all are to be involved in the calling and nurturing of new Christians as the baptising community. How this focus stands in relation to being the eucharistic community is picked up in the last chapter.

Another misunderstanding that should be referred to is the tendency at times to regard the process as overly difficult. In Chapter 3 I mentioned the view which some clergy and lay leaders have expressed, namely, that the process seems too difficult. This misunderstanding derives, I believe, from a failure to capture the basic point that as a process leaders must 'go with the flow' and not require or look for a programmatic guide. What is needed is a grasp of a basic sense of the process and then gain understanding by experiencing it – good acquaintance comes in the doing in which leadership is supported and mentored during the first experience of the process.

The first time I was in a team to lead the process I had a mentor whom I spoke to on the phone every fortnight. Due to the 'going with flow' nature of group meetings, leadership often meant 'going by the seat of one's pants'. Often what was planned for a session did not eventuate due to the issues raised by the group at the time. I needed these phone conversations for support in my first year. As clergy we are accustomed to being in control. Some clergy may reject the approach for this reason. At this point we can be invited to review our opinion and entertain embarking on the adventure of the process with others.

The Spirit's invitation is to go to the edge and sit. A colleague of mine says the process is in fact simple: all we need to do is proceed in the group with people's questions (and at times help them explore what they are really asking) on the one hand, and on the other hand turn to reflection on scripture. In this way the process actually WORKS!

There are different styles of leadership. The style of the colleague just mentioned is 'high inductive'. Some leadership models proceed well with more input, that is, with more deductive elements. There is a range of styles of leadership, therefore, in which we are free to develop our own. To be mentored during the first time of leading is vital and helps in the evolution of one's style.

Joy of the Church

The phrase "the joy of the Church" appears in one of St John Chrysostom's talks, his Catechetical Orations of the fourth century, as he led the catechumens of the time to their commitment at the Easter font in the city of Antioch. He was directing the phrase to the catechumens – "You all are the joy of the Church." Indeed it is often the sense that a congregation today has, after a few years of becoming familiar with the process, that to witness the faith and awareness, the clear decision and courage of those to be baptised and confirmed as they approach the font, is to encounter a great measure of joy in the local church in its centring on being a community of initiation.

The joy that both the newly initiated and the congregation may experience needs to be safe-guarded by the process being sufficiently long for journey and conversion as well as to ensure that the catechumens begin to settle in their faith life and to be truly oriented to ministry and service. The time frames suggested in this chapter may at times need to be lengthened. As a Roman Catholic commentator has written:

> *The time spent in the catechumenate should be long enough for the conversion and faith of the catechumens to be strong. By their formation in the entire Christian life and a sufficiently*

prolonged probation the catechumens are properly initiated into the mysteries of salvation … they are led into the life of faith, worship and charity.[30]

End note: Resources for using the 'Easter Journey':

In the Australian Anglican Church the publication, Using the Catechumenate in Australia is available from the Anglican Diocese of Adelaide Education Office. For a review of the implementation of the process over its first fifteen years of use within that national church, the report entitled, What do you Seek? in available form the Anglican Information Office, Anglican Centre, Melbourne. Consult national, regional or diocesan education offices for particular denominational resources.

AFRICAN BIBLE STUDY METHOD:

A three fold reading of a passage after which participants give their own response (or may choose to say "pass"). A short discussion follows after all have responded. A different member of the group reads the passage aloud each time.

Before the first reading group members are asked to respond with what strikes them, mentioning a phase, a word, a sense of something. Before the 2nd reading members are asked to respond with what connects in the passage with their life. For the 3rd reading they are asked what they can do/act upon. The exercise often ends with the person next to another saying a short prayer, which could be a word or phrase, for that person.

30 Barbara Hixon, *RCIA Spirituality*, Resource Publications, Inc. 1997.

CHAPTER 6

IN THE NAME OF THE FATHER: GOD'S CARE, GOD'S WORLD

These next three chapters describe the outcomes that occur during the stages of the process as they been have practiced and observed especially in parts of Australia. This is a sharing of the fruits of experience as leadership teams and participants have involved themselves in the journey to commitment and community.

In the Name of the Trinity

The invocation of the Trinity at the point of baptismal immersion provides an image of seeing what is discovered in the process. The invocation – in the name of the Father and of the Son and of the Holy Spirit – summarily gives expression to a person's movement into God's life, into communion with God the Holy Trinity. As we shall see a method of describing the outcomes of the stages corresponds, or can readily be associated with, each of the divine Persons and in particular with qualities or attributes associated with each.

As participants progress in the 'Easter Journey' they encounter these ways or attributes of God. As I have thought about the pattern of experiences in the process, it does approximate I believe, to a 'good fit' between attributes traditionally ascribed to each of the Persons and what takes place in the stages of the process. There are three attributes of each of the Persons of the Trinity that are focussed upon in each of the stages:

Inquiry:	the Father: God's Care, God's world
Formation:	the Son: Word, Healer, Saviour
Reflection (after Easter):	the Holy Spirit: Companioning, Belonging, Gifts.

It is to be noted that having described the 'good fit' it is not an exact 'fit'. The 'Easter Journey' by virtue of being a 'flowing process' and not a programmatic, curriculum oriented endeavour, indicates to us that the ways or attributes of God mentioned will be discovered and related to throughout the process in all of the stages. The realisations and awakenings that occur for participants, for example, to do with God's Care or the Saviour, are not confined exclusively to the stage designated to it. Nevertheless, it is true to say, that it is within the specific stages that the realisations and awakenings regarding the respective themes *mainly* take place.

The understanding of the Trinity in Celtic spirituality can help us see how this manner of seeing the process outcomes is appropriate here. Celtic spirituality enables us to see our lives *within the embrace* of the Three Persons in one God. Indeed it enables us to see the world and all of nature in God's embrace. It is within this embrace that we experience the redemptive ways of God with us and in us, such as God's care, healing and gifts. This appreciation of God's trinitarian nature in relation to ourselves and the world can be contrasted to the overly objectifying understanding with which many of us in the West have grown up. The habit of objectifying the Persons of the Godhead as observable – 'out there' or 'in front of us', as it were, 'on the table' – was frequently practiced in sermons and Sunday schools in previous decades. Objectified images were used to attempt to *explain* the mystery of the Trinity, such as comparing God to an apple having three parts, core, flesh, skin. We may now suspect that such an analogy is somehow wrong-placed and verges on the ridiculous. This objectifying is in truth not helpful.

The Celtic tradition stands more in continuity with the ancient Church than with the Victorian and twentieth century Church. Only with great hesitancy did the church fathers in their theological tomes use analogies to point to the (incomprehensible) verity of the Holy Trinity, to the God who is mysteriously and intimately present as well as transcendent.

The Celtic habit of using circle – or dance – like prayers follows directly from their understanding of God the Trinity. They can help us see our place in the cosmic, communal and personal embrace of the Divine:

In the love of the Father
In the light of Christ
In the leading of the Spirit,
We place ourselves today.

Around thee twine the Three
The One the Trinity
The Father bind his love
The Son tie his salvation
The Spirit wrap his power
Make you new creation
Around thee twine the Three
The encircling of the Trinity[31]

People find that the 'Easter Journey' is a way of coming to know God through experience, scripture and community: not primarily coming to know *about* God. The latter is an activity that can be pursued secondarily, after, and not before, spiritual encounters occur. The use of the personal journal maintains an important role in this regard, as participants respond in their own ways to scripture, inputs and sharing. The triune nature of

God becomes 'learnt' therefore through participation in the formational process akin to the Celtic way of praying. This approach was the way of the Church in the first centuries.

Hence the moment of baptism at the font holds much in meaning and experience. The words that the celebrant says while immersing or pouring the water over those being baptised, "I baptise you (*person's name*) in the name of the Father and of the Son and of the Holy Spirit", gains a particular character in terms of all that precedes the sacramental event. The action gathers up the journey to grace and in grace which the individuals have encountered thus far and will further encounter after being baptised.

Group Forming

Let us go back to the beginning of the process. Imagine you are a seeker and are prepared to join the first stage of the group. You become an inquirer. You are not normally a group contributor and are shy at first to participate actively. However, listening to the questions, concerns and a few of other people's stories encourages you to feel able to make your own contribution. Early on, a culture of 'inquiry solidarity' emerges which includes the companions (not yet allocated one-to-one to seekers). You learn months later that a key piece of advice given to companions for their role is to participate not as church people who 'know a lot' but as fellow learners who are in touch with a healthy "love and hate of the Church"[32].You like that! You are able to sense an environment of trust in which something spiritual may well grow.

Self-Authority

Early in the process many inquirers will make judgments for themselves regarding what is true for them without reference to any authority outside themselves. Self-authority is the disposition of the individualised westerner. The category of the 'spiritual' will be a part of the world-view of some seekers, being included in the language of various New Age avenues that they have been exposed to or simply as part of an amorphous youth cultural view-point. Whilst holding some form of spiritual values these don't have the status of authority to change life fundamentally. The New Age movement is not a unified philosophy or system that requires a basic change in outlook by those who enter into its wide domain. Rather it is a 'grab bag' of various traditions, ancient and modern.[33] As a movement it encourages diffuse thinking, a lack of making distinctions. Overall, however, it needs to be taken seriously by the Church, "sustaining, as it does, the rumour of God rather than any clarity about God".[34] Here is an opportunity for a form of evangelisation.

Various deep experiences that Christians could broadly call 'spiritual' in that they appear oriented and close to Christian truths, are often in the background of seekers' lives. The walking of the Santiago de Compostela pilgrimage as Coehlo did before his return to Christianity, exemplifies this point. Equally, many experiences of nature, of music, of love and friendship, of undeserved felt-care, of survival and emergence from trial and tragedy, can also be said to hold something spiritual ... all these become the ground for reflection as to "what is at stake for me" ... "where is real meaning?". These are examples of what was mentioned earlier in referring to "prevenient grace": Calvin's term for God's work in a person before Christian conversion.

Opening Up

If then self-authority stands as a kind of starting-point it need not remain as it is for very long. It is in fact rarely a certain, confident kind of authority. What is discovered in relation to this condition in today's western culture, is a gentle widening in the person in the context of the Christian ambience of the group. Relationships can open out. For those who have found themselves to have a somewhat isolated orientation, often it is found that the self broadens. In this, as in other contexts, relationships tend to rescue the stance of self-authority from participants feeling negative or even destructive of themselves or of others.

Group life in its relational aspect can soon bring to bear a questioning of the position of self-authority as individuals are genuinely listened to and heard. Group bonds form. When companions are allocated to seekers at the end of the Inquiry stage they need to have a degree of empathy and of gentle challenge in their association with their group partners in order to help them progress.

Personal stories are shared and connections made. The journal becomes a close 'friend' of each participant as it is utilised for various jottings. Looking back to what was noted in earlier sessions the journal invites each person to build on questions and insights then posed. Periods of silence in the group are helpful for people to muse over their journal notes.

Providence and Purpose

Then, into the ring a scriptural story is pitched. It is about some aspects of God's way with the people of the past. In this environment of the first series of meetings a sense of providence begins to emerge, of God's care of people. At first there may be members of the group who do not find traditional talk of God easy. They may be happier with a kind of broadly defined sense the 'spirit' or "the Spirit" – part and parcel of a common, vague, culturally-bound agnosticism. A starting point in religious comprehension often takes place through the experience of the quality of care in the group and the witness of scripture in terms of the providence of God or of Jesus' compassion. Often in the Australian context some participants bring an image of God as a harsh judge acquired from their Sunday School days. An invitation to revisit this image can be extended in order to see alternatives.

As questions and concerns are discussed, in addition to perceiving God's care for persons, a sense of purpose in life and of the world having some goodly intended direction, comes into view. If God created all things then the world surely is not meant to be 'for nothing' or 'for a bad end'. This perception of purpose is sensed as important; albeit not necessarily at this point of the process is this clearly defined in terms of belief or doctrine.

The sense of purpose on the personal level is also awakened through group reflection on participants' own lives. Reflection here may begin simply with people sharing an aspect of their lives that is significant to them. The group is asked to listen attentively and respond sensitively. In the second stage of the process often a life map exercise is used in which participants draws a graph of their life thus far, depicting it, for example, below and above a horizontal line that delineates the years passed. They are asked to highlight a few spots on the drawing as significant parts of their life journey. Shared reflection on this exercise can lead to a deepened appreciation of their own lives and especially of a sense of 'the redemptive' in which good things happened during or after bad times; alternatively, this sense occurs for them presently in the group process. God then can begin to be named; what begins to be discovered is that God's Story intersects with people's story and the more we enter into this intersection the more free and purposeful we become.

Both by being introduced to scriptural and life reflection we can say that in the group's Inquiry stage, and flowing on from it, the focus is on God's providence and purpose – in Trinitarian terms on God the Father, God's parental care, God's world.

Finally, in summarising the kinds of issues that emerge in this phase, the question of evil arises: '*why* bad things happen to good people?'. This area of discussion is about the fact that evil manifests itself powerfully in the world. This fundamental question or issue is often held and kept held in the process: kept alive, for at this point there may not be the tools for a sufficient reply to it. Here is an instance of the leadership being prepared to live with a question, allowing it the seriousness that is its due and letting it be addressed in time as people explore and reframe it.

Let there be storytelling,
Let there be questioning,
Let there be communities of faith,
Let there be Tradition,
Let there be conversion,
Let there be celebration, and
Let there be ministries.[35]

31 Two prayers from David Adam's books *The Open Gate* and *The Edge of Glory*.

32 See the suggested characteristics for a companion in Anne Mc Ellicott's *The Catechumenal Process*, Church Hymnal Corporation 1990 p.103.

33 Wesley Carr, *Manifold Wisdom, Christians in the New Age*, SPCK 1991 p.80.

34 Carr.

35 From the North American Catechumenate website 2004: www.catechumenate.org

CHAPTER 7

… AND OF THE SON: WORD, HEALER, SAVIOUR

The group journey to Easter involves responding to gospel stories through which participants look closely at the Jesus of the gospels. Gospel encounter is especially a part of the second, the Formational stage, and is about being prepared to grow in faith and begin to see oneself in discipleship with others.

Often group members may not be very confident of what is involved in this step but are nevertheless willing to venture forward. It can seem like a big jump from the level of understanding and growth arrived at in the first stage. In this chapter I wish to suggest that the second stage is closely related to gaining a relationship with Jesus as Son of God and especially in his way with us as:

Word,
Healer and
Saviour.

In association with each of these categories of who Jesus is for us I shall describe three 'Easter Journey' situations as each took placed in group sessions. These situations will convey the kinds of outcomes that occur in the movement towards Easter and commitment.

Word

The first situation is representative of the manner in which group members find their own way in faith discovery through the gospel encounter method, that is, through encounter with the 'Word'.

> A MIRACLE OF WAKING UP
>
> *Alan had liked attending Inquiry with the sharing of aspects of his life story and listening to others. As a scientific minded, matter-of-fact personality, he had taken much of his life journey and its significance in relation to himself for granted. He began to realise this. He sensed that in moving forward in the group he would have difficulties believing much in the gospel accounts yet he was prepared to be open-minded.*
>
> *During a session in which the passage of Jesus' stilling of the storm with the disciples in the boat was read, he exclaimed that he didn't believe in the miraculous. An elderly parishioner in the group, a companion, replied, "Alan, you don't have to believe that Jesus actually overpowered nature, just look at what you can get out of the story!" After some pondering he found something in the passage that engaged him personally. "I'm asleep in the boat like the disciples", he shared. "I am out of touch with so much in my life."*

Later, the leader commended the parishioner for her reply to Alan, especially since he knew that as a devout person she herself probably ascribed firmly to the belief that Jesus possessed miraculous powers. She had met Alan 'in his moment'; intellectual belief at this point was not the most important issue; what was important for him was personally accessing something of significance in the story as the text conveyed it.

Alan continued in 'the Journey' as largely a 'waking up' pilgrimage, owning and valuing his story, seeing spiritual or 'charged' aspects of it. Members of the group named "grace" at times as a category that his inner ear heard and was able to receive. In this way the avenue of faith opened before him.

The main point about this situation is that, with the use of the scriptural method, people are often enabled to find their own way towards and into personal faith. Alan was challenged out of his habit of staying in his 'head space'. Almost universally people find in gospel encounter an aspect of the text speaking to them in a manner that surprises them and which awakens something deep within them. Later, they begin to appreciate the place of the Word of God, in the life of the Church. Here is a beginning.

Healer

The second situation is about the inner healing nature of encountering Jesus in gospel text:

SINNER WOMAN STIRS UP COMPASSION

A group was asked to share responses to the story of Jesus dining at a Pharisee's house. The story describes how a woman, "a sinner" comes to Jesus to anoint his feet and wipe them with her hair and her tears. The Pharisee objects to Jesus' loving acceptance of the woman's action (Lk.7:36-50).

In response, one person was moved by the emotion of the event, the outpouring of the woman and simply wanted to sit with her own sense of wonder as somehow she felt being part of the story. Later she associated her response with a movement in her towards devotion and worship.

Another person discovered a sense of unworthiness, not liking what he saw inside himself but also becoming curious and mindful of the acceptance of Jesus. A third person looked at the warmth and compassion of Jesus in the face of the host's objections and acknowledged that he was being stirred to be more compassionate in his life.

People in the group responded to the passage variously; they responded to Jesus as the key figure in the story differently. Furthermore, in sharing their responses participants were able to minister an insight that was helpful to others in the group. In each of responses mentioned above a path of inner healing opened up for the particular participants in the form of what was needed for their lives at the time.

As sessions proceed the Word of God, God speaking in and through the scriptures, becomes a lived truth for participants. 'Jesus as healer' becomes a believed tenet of faith especially through the encounters with the text that centre on him and the relationship with Jesus that ensues. The companions' sharing of their faith in Christ especially through their own times of suffering supports this discovery.

In this Formation phase issues of unworthiness in the guise of habitual problems or forms of addiction can arise. Participants are encouraged to acknowledge these in confidentiality, to talk to their companions and if needed to the priest or minister. As Easter approaches these and any difficulties individuals have, are prayed for, sometimes in the form of a small group liturgy which may include anointing.

Saviour

Group life progresses to look at the question of suffering and evil. The topic of the crucifixion of Jesus is introduced or comes up in its own way. In looking at gospel accounts the topic of redemption is discussed. The following situation has some salient features about finding Christ as Saviour:

LAST MINUTE ENLIGHTENMENT

As a young adult, Sid had spent some years attending Buddhist teaching. It had brought a strong sense of peacefulness to his life. He was a slightly reluctant group attender at first because

> *of not having good memories of Christianity through the private school version of religion he had been subjected to as a teenager.*
>
> *Sid valued the exercises of scriptural reflection. He began to see Jesus as Teacher of enlightenment, similar to the Buddha. He knew, however, there was more to Christianity than seeing Jesus as Teacher and as Easter and the time of commitment approached this thought bothered him.*

Trusting in the Spirit's working in the process and seeing a genuine openness in Sid, the priest advised him to continue and be open to what he would receive in and through Holy Week. While attending the Good Friday service 'the penny dropped'. The message in its freshness was conveyed to him that Christ died out of love for us and all humanity: Jesus is more than Teacher but is Saviour as well. After further discussion Sid re-affirmed his faith on Easter morning.

Considerable discernment was required to encourage Sid to keep looking for more in the process and then to proceed to his commitment on Easter morning. The important step in his growth of faith happened on Good Friday, just two days before the great Easter morning. Facilitating the 'Easter Journey', 'going with the flow', certainly is a 'seat-of-pants' affair in which leaders are called to let the Spirit work.

The situation points to the fact that people's growth in faith can occur in many and varied ways: through pondering a piece of art, through silence, through liturgy, a spoken word in season. A good adult initiation process must avail itself of various approaches and resources as given to us as a part of God's good Creation. In this case, it was the effect of liturgy, of being among the worshipping community on an important day, that was determinative in helping a group member move into a confessing faith.

Furthermore, the situation points to the need for those in the initiation process, whether to be baptised, confirmed or to re-affirm their faith, to gain a sense of Christ's death being, as John Wesley put it, for me – personally, as well as for the whole world. The 'for me' and 'for us' nature of the death of Christ is about grace in suffering, the forgiveness of sins and is also about being on the pathway to eternal life in his merciful love.

The three situations recorded in this chapter are about people finding faith and growing in faith. Conversion takes place in several ways. In the first situation, there was an encountering of the Word as an inspired word, timely and in season, in which the participant responded to the text. The life-giving 'word' that comes to a person in this type of scriptural engagement can be literally a written part of the text or can be 'beneath' the written text as a form of sensing something special. Each is a participation in the ministry of Christ the Word in the community of faith and is a response to the Word.

In the second situation, an account of a group response to the passage of the women who comes to anoint Jesus' feet, various insights were shared that were of healing significance to each person. This account is indicative of the belief coming into view that Jesus is the living, active healer especially of our emotions and wills.

In the third situation, namely, of making sense of the crucifixion and of Jesus being more than a teacher, the importance of discovering the salvific nature of Christianity was shown, namely, that Jesus is Saviour. Not only does this truth need to be found but what is illustrative here is that it was discovered, as other truths can be discovered, by participating in the worshipping life of the community at an appropriate time. A spiritual leader and the group accompanied the person to be a sounding board and to encourage.

As group sessions explore the latter part of the life of Jesus and especially his trial and crucifixion, the topics of suffering, death and evil are reflected upon in relation to Jesus' ministry during these events. Evil is exposed for what it is in the violent, unjust death of Jesus and is therefore to be resisted in our discipleship.

Following Christ as Word, Healer and Saviour comes into special focus in the Lenten season. As Easter approaches, in taking up seriously the way of discipleship, participants are asked to attend to their own blockages or resistances to entering fully into this new life. The traditional word for this focus "the scrutinies" is still maintained in the Roman Catholic RCIA process. Prayer and encouragement are provided as companions and congregation acknowledge their needs and weaknesses. Dying and rising with Christ becomes a grace-filled reality as all are summoned to leave the dead wood of aspects of the old life behind and tend the fresh shoots of the new life. Both congregation and journey group look at the promises of the baptismal covenant as that covenant is presented and as all present are renewed in it at Easter. In this manner the resurrection of the Son of God, Word, Healer and Saviour is affirmed and celebrated.

CHAPTER 8

… AND OF THE HOLY SPIRIT: COMPANIONING, BELONGING, GIFTS

The 'Easter Journey' can rightly be understood as a journey in the Holy Spirit, the third Person of the Trinity – a process in which participants find spiritual surprises and challenges. This dimension of the 'Easter Journey' that is 'of the Holy Sprit' is a source of wonder to the leaders and often participants as they ponder situations that emerge. On reflection these situations are realised to be all to do with the mystery of God's grace in the Person of "the Incognito One" (Bonhoeffer's phrase), the Holy Spirit.

This quality of group life includes the times when the group may come to breaking point through members getting in touch with points of suffering in their lives and with which there appears to be no way out. Then, in time, a break-through, a healing moment is given and the person or the group can move on. Included here are phases of group malaise, usually based on fear. As the group discusses and explores, often new courage is found. Being watchful, caring and flexible as leaders assists in the Spirit's creative work.

The nurture of adults in the process in which the Spirit of God is at work is largely focussed on three aspects or qualities of the Holy Spirit:

companioning,
belonging and
the cultivation of gifts for ministry.

In the New Testament letters the work of the Holy Spirit is largely described in terms of bringing about Christian communities and building them up in terms of these three qualities.

Companioning

As 'Journey' members move into the Formational stage each person is given a companion. Quite often there are unlikely pairings decided by the leadership team in aligning an inquirer to a companion. The team is encouraged not only to consider commonalities but also some differences as a basis for alignment. People's journeys in the group are enriched in this way. The journeying together, meeting weekly over coffee or at crèche or during the business lunch hour … enables 'chewings' over the previous session or over whatever else comes up, and therefore brings a sense of grounded-ness to the process for each person. The Spirit can only work with what is – what is in each person not what is not!

Short stories of companionship are provided in this book in some of 'the incidents' that begin each of the chapters in the next section.

At Easter when the companions place their hands on the shoulder of their friends to be baptised, confirmed or to reaffirm their faith, the *companione* – literally, eating bread together – is driven home to them. The friendships crafted in the Spirit often last many years as the two continue to worship together Sunday by Sunday in the assembled breaking of the bread.

Belonging

Belonging is quite powerfully discovered by many in the process. After the gospel encounter (described in the last chapter) based on the woman who comes to Jesus and wipes his feet with her tears, the session moved into a second segment:

> NEW SPACE, VARIED RESPONSES
>
> *The leader invited participants to move to the sanctuary from the back of the church were they had been seated together. The group went to stand around the altar. A circle was formed and after a period of brief silence each person was asked what it was like to stand in the space. "Special", "uneasy", "good", "I'm in a holy space", "a strange feeling of 'I think I somehow belong here'", were some of the responses.*

Since this exercise took place immediately after the particular scriptural exercise at hand the group members were able to make the connection between the affection between Jesus and the woman in the gospel story on the one hand, and, a spiritual significance about being around the altar together on the other hand. The former was about a profound acceptance and the latter was about beginning to belong. Just as the first exercise led to the second, so too, acceptance leads to belonging.

The session was held fairly early in the journey process. As the group members were invited to gather around the altar they became aware of a sense of belonging. Even with the response "uneasy" there was a threshold querying about the sense and importance of belonging.

When group members commence the Formation stage they are urged to attend Sunday services and to discuss in the group meetings their thoughts about being a part of the corporate worship. Here in this session members of the group were able to access a sense of belonging not just based on an assessment of 'how I am welcomed on a Sunday morning' but rather as based on Jesus as the central figure regarding the issue of belonging. It is he who welcomes and establishes that seekers belong. The

Church into which each person is welcomed from its edge, is build on Christ's grace. Belonging hence is not primarily brought about in a humanistic fashion – by the efforts of stirring up congregational friendliness – but by grace. It is the outworking of that grace that creates the welcoming environment of belonging. The outcomes of the group session described here is just one example of how this development can occur.

Christians hopefully grow in their sense of belonging in a community. Usually the process is gradual; so it is for participants in the 'Easter Journey'. After Easter or near Pentecost the congregation will often invite the newly baptised and confirmed to share aspects of their faith journey as it has occurred in the group process. Being received into the congregation warmly and with special-ness nearly always stands out in these reflections. The need to find community, instanced by Peter's story in the introduction, is so acute in urban, western society. At the same time there is often the suspicion in the mind of the outsider that 'this congregation may well be a closed shop'. Both these factors can be overcome in the movement and the break-throughs into belonging. The Holy Spirit is always prompting us to bring about open community and to enable people to enter the community in their own way. As we continue to hear the Gospel in community, Jesus' commitment to welcoming and incorporating those on the edge into his new community, begin to stick and be acted upon.

In the 'Journey' sessions that take place after Easter, participants' sense of belonging is deepened in being oriented to the Word, in the emphasis on life-long participation in the sacraments and in the invitation to take up avenues of ministry and mission.

In Christian terms belonging has a paradoxical meaning: we are drawn into belonging to a community which by virtue of being a community is bounded, inside with fellow community members; at the same time we are drawn into its domain to be spiritually and radically oriented to the outsider, to the edge, to the other.

Gifts

In the approximately eight month period of the 'Easter Journey' group members naturally come to know each other well. Late in the process awareness of the gifts of each person comes to the fore. Gifts such as caring, prayer, listening and discernment, passion for justice, sometimes hidden to others, reveal themselves slowly and can be named. The gifts of the Holy Spirit in the New Testament are looked at and group members are asked to discern where their gifts for ministry may lie in the faith community. Equally, the discerning of where gifts and call for ministry lie in the family, at work and in the local and wider community of the world, are explored, kindled and affirmed.

Group life is frequently a precious commodity today. A thanksgiving celebration at Pentecost, at the end of the process, encourages participants to take their place in the life of the Christian community and to bring the group to closure. The celebration may include a commissioning for ministry. Whilst closure can happen smoothly a particular group may feel reluctant to terminate meeting together. The bonds and shared journey remain precious in people's minds. The sense of being a part of the Body of Christ has been witnessed primarily in group life rather than in the wider parish. Furthermore, the heavy, institutional characteristics of church life are sometimes a hurdle to get over and so group members sometimes feel the need to hang onto their smaller unit of belonging.

Respect for this predicament by parish leaders is required. As the group acknowledges the gifted-ness of its members, creative ways of helping participants gradually find their way fully into the faith community can be facilitated. The discerning of each person's ministry, including possibly starting some new ministry in or outside the faith community, can take time. It is often when this step is carefully taken that group members are content to move on.

Challenge to Institutional Life

The influence of the 'Easter Journey' in the guise of the topics mentioned in these last three chapters can stand as a challenge to those features of institutionalism that probably have not been critiqued enough within the contemporary Christian community. We find ourselves on 'the cusp of Christendom' with the legacy of so much institutional weight of the past. 'Journey' members will have freshly experienced qualities of the Christian life in the group that may not appear as strongly present in the church community that they have joined, qualities such as – shared attentiveness to the Word, encounters of inner healing, the quality of companionship.

In these circumstances they will tend to ask questions of the community regarding why these qualities are inhibited and why greater opportunities are not given for the outcomes of the 'Journey' process to address present parish priorities. Questions can be asked such as:

- does the parish give enough of a priority to the opening up of its life to facilitate the making of new Christians? …
- how important to church members and to the leadership, in comparison to other goals, is the devoting of congregational energy to the edge? …
- what defines the dominant culture of the parish and how open is it? …

When such questions are raised, albeit difficult ones, are they not in fact questions that are inspired by the Holy Spirit?

CHAPTER 9

PASCAL PARTICIPATION

The drama of adult baptism at Easter as a culmination of the 'Journey' is not dependent upon any sense of theatre on the part of the worship leaders. Rather, it arises from those composite factors that function prior to Easter: emerging faith through the months of preparation, congregational and group bonds of fellowship, and a sense of expectation and wonder. It is on this basis that the sacrament does its work. I wrote these lines after one Easter morning:

EASTER MOMENT

Bowing for baptism, time of decision and grace –
heart descending
into the waters below, pure, awakening –
met with waters above falling, lavishing –
Holy Spirit around, God embracing;
decision decided … … risking
to walk and stop, turn back?
stop, run, walk and walk on;
act of fire and love encountered
not to be forgotten;
bond never to be broken;
now on the Way – momented.

To journey on – to be fed at the Table –
of sacrifice, the offering
of Christ's life and mine in him,
walking the walk of the Son
in the Spirit to the Father.

We have seen that the walk to the font at Easter is accompanied by learning, change and growth that can be associated with the Persons of the Trinity, the life of God into which people are baptised.

Aiden Kavanagh, in his important work, *The Shape of Baptism,*[36] describes the tradition in which the Church's preparing and baptising of candidates (catechumens) at Easter enacts the fullness of the baptismal experience for the whole Church:

Baptism in its fullness is the primary liminal experience during which the Church is shaped each pascal season into a community of equals in one Body of neither Jew or Greek, master or slave, male or female – prepared to see fresh and new God's grace … In its catechumens the Church passes in Christ from death to life each year at the Pasca … "[37]

In the spirit of the New Testament, approaching baptism is about turning to Jesus Christ, repenting of sin and accepting the new life offered. At the heart of the New Testament's teaching on baptism is the mystery of our participation in the death and resurrection of Christ: 'pascal participation'. "Pascal" means to do with the *Pasca*, the event of the Passover in Jewish history, and so, in Christian terms, "pascal" refers to the passing over from death to life, from an old life to a new life in Christ.

Furthermore, as Kavanagh reminds us, this baptismal passover involves the incorporation of new people presumably from various walks of life. The sacramental transition means that there is the shaping and renewing of the community as the community of equals annually. The baptised community of equals in Christian understanding[38] images and bears witness to the new humanity under the Reign of God that Christ inaugurated.

It is the notion of the pascal mystery and our participation in this mystery that I want to explore in this chapter. It holds a central importance for an appreciation of the adult initiation way in its integration of a life-centred, Gospel-oriented process and a companioned journey to Easter, with the celebration of the resurrection of Jesus being the climax of the journey and of decision, the point of Holy Baptism. It is in this corporate journey that the topic of suffering poignantly arises, is made sense of and finds its avenue of transformation.

New Life in Holy Baptism

To explore this dimension we firstly should clarify how the pascal mystery is a part of baptism. In gathering up much of the discussion of the last three chapters I see the immersion in water at baptism as representing deepening levels of meaning and participation. In modern Anglican practice there are three levels which correspond to the questions and responses made by the candidates for baptism.[39] The description given to each level of meaning is in accordance with what the 'Journey' participants' experience. Hence the Easter baptismal rite is a gathering up of this experience into graced decision and commitment.

The diagram on the next page depicts baptism as the once-and-for-all-time event in a person's life in which centrally there is a letting go of the old life to take up the new life: the great movement down and up from the old to the new. A., B. and C. depict deepening levels of meaning. In the 'Journey' process A. represents the turning to Christ in which participants orient and begin to trust the Jesus of gospel encounter and of the faith stories that they hear. In B. there is the repentance of changing one's mind and life direction with the hearing of the call of Christ. In C. the difficulties of one's own life are faced and the difficulties of the world around us. This is the level par excellence of entering into Christ's pascal mystery, namely, into the area of darkness where in shared trust he accompanies us to new life and light.

New Life *in* Holy Baptism

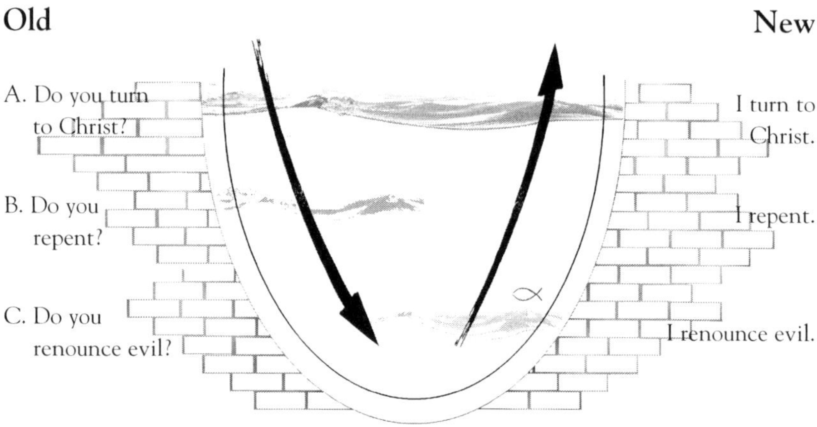

A. Turning to see and get in touch with the healing liberating Jesus.
B. Making the decision to change direction – change of mind – to follow Jesus.
C. Facing the big difficulties in myself and in the world, trusting for discipleship.

In coming to the Easter font these meanings coalesce in the baptismal celebration It is an event in which the whole local community shares and, as Kavanagh points out, it is best understood and practiced annually as the renewal of the community in its baptismal foundation. Dying and rising with Christ becomes the pattern of life's journey from now on.

Living the Pascal Mystery

In the initiation process people are introduced to the Jesus of the gospels, to the one claimed to be the Son of God who identifies with struggling, suffering human beings from the point of his own baptism.

Inquirers learn of this solidarity as it connects with them and their lives through the sharing of stories and scripture. This is particularly true when a few members of the group are opened up in the process to some powerfully difficult issues in their lives. Each person is encouraged, especially through the bible study method, to take small steps themselves in the path of healing and to let God do the rest. For some people the pathway may be particularly deep as they confront such difficulties as grief or wounds of childhood. Gradually, over the weeks of the process, the miracle of new life and purpose somehow is given; the gift is accompanied by the trusting prayer of those around them.

Personal difficulties are to be understood in the process as centrally a part of life, the grist of living. They are not to be avoided by the maintenance of fear, by drugs or by pretence. As Easter approaches they are to be seen in relation to the death, entombment and resurrection of Christ. By means of new-found faith Christ takes hold of us and leads us through. Sometimes the entombment, in which there is inner darkness and no movement of life occurs, feels very long. Yet the invitation and the urging is to continue with promise of healing at hand.

A profound moment in Martin Luther King's life is illustrative at this point. In 1955 during the Montgomery Bus Boycott King was arrested for the first time. In jail at midnight he was awakened by a hate phone call. As he sat thinking of the dangers to his family (some days later his house was burnt down) he had his first profound religious experience. As he wrote in *Stride towards Freedom*:

At that moment I experienced the presence of the divine as I had never before. It seemed as though I could hear the quiet assurance of an inner voice saying, "Stand up for righteousness, stand up for truth and God will be at your side forever."

This point in King's life is an example of what many people face: the impossibility of resurrection in dark, cell-like conditions, inner or outer … then, in time, amidst inner wrestling and anguish mingled with faint moments of trust and hope, spiritual release is given, the intimation of resurrection … God raises the dead to life.

Group members who don't go through these deep experiences are nevertheless asked to be in solidarity with those that do. All therefore learn this fundamental dimension of baptism, namely, that there is with Christ nothing so dark and deep that cannot be touched by his healing grace. He enters – eis[40] – into the watery chaos of the life of this world for all time, as Mark's description of Christ's baptism reveals.

Seeing their suffering as shared by Christ, the way forward is to rise *with him*. As he does not shirk his trial and dies in crucifixion in the face of all that is evil in the world, so we are called to make a stand in his strength: to die to sin in ourselves and in the world, and to rise to be his instruments of peace. Having entered *into* the watery chaos of life the risen Jesus is ever present to bring his followers through suffering and trial.

This dying and rising is on-going. It is a core aspect of the Christian life and is the focus of our involvement in the eucharist, the sharing in the broken body and poured our blood of Christ. The eucharist is then the other great sacrament to which the newly baptised must share in and do so regularly.

St Paul plumbs the depth of the pascal mystery in chapter three of his letter to the Philippians:

I want to know Christ and the power of his resurrection and the sharing of his suffering by becoming like him in his death. (v.11) and,

He will transform the body of our humiliation that it may be conformed to the body of his glory (v.21).

Also in his letter to the Romans he writes:

If we are children, we are heirs as well: heirs of God and co-heirs with Christ, sharing in his sufferings so as to share his glory (8:17).

Reflecting on this theme of pascal participation as it manifests itself in the adult initiation process leads to the following points being made:

1. Christ's solidarity in suffering with us is reflected in the role of the companions. The role of the companions is to encourage the other person to look carefully and honestly at their lives in association with the gospel passages and not to give up when the going is difficult. Companions are urged to pray daily for their 'Journey' partner. A key aspect of this role is to help them see that God accepts them as they are, to come as they are on the way of discipleship.
2. Experiencing suffering in whatever ways leads to a thirst for and openness to prayer – avenues of prayer that satisfy the deeper recesses of the human spirit. The prayer of silence becomes a form of prayer that many group participants take a strong interest in.
3. Awareness of addictive tendencies, as they are present in all of us, can come into focus. These do not have to be the well-known forms of addiction like drugs, alcohol or gambling, but can be habits like dominance or being overly submissive to others or clinging to possessions. Turning to God and taking small steps to act in some way of response to the Gospel becomes the invitation to each person within the healing path. This is an example of the pascal way in terms of 'letting go' to let God work. As a consequence participants grow in a deeper knowledge of themselves; in other words they discover that the path of self-knowledge is inherent in the call and way of discipleship.

4. The Holy Spirit continually acts in the area of personal work and trust. The Spirit is seen as God's attentiveness to hold, renew and strengthen each person through avenues of vulnerability.
5. The great celebration of Easter, the pascal feast, provides the unique, evocative, lived and shared focus for the entry into this way of life. The celebration is discovered to be devoid of humanly contrived hype, having a rare, spiritual buoyancy, a deep fellowship and awe.
6. The habit of niceness, often prevalent in church culture, is confronted by the orientation towards developed honesty and faith sharing of group members as suffering is taken seriously. Gradually this culture element can be turned upside down as people face life and its truths more squarely. In turn, people are enabled to be more genuinely light hearted and joyful in the company of each other.
7. Having exposure to the needy in the community brings a discovery of Christ's presence with the poor. The discovery involves a 'letting go' of preconceived – superior or ignorant – notions about the disadvantaged and leads to a fresh engagement, seeing them in gospel terms as brothers and sisters.
8. The gift of tears, traditionally in Eastern Orthodoxy associated with baptism and seen as a spiritual gift, is often displayed in the initiation process and at Easter, as sorrow in joy and joy in sorrow.

People in the process therefore learn the way of Christ, that is, an acceptance to be vulnerable as those in the gospels he spent so much time with, and to be vulnerable together. Somehow this is the path of grace. An English monk once said on a television program, 'Blessed are the cracked for they let the light in!'

A further perspective comes into view as all these considerations are centred on the suffering, death and resurrection of Jesus. A sense of his passionate concern for the welfare of all peoples, for peace and justice in every corner of the globe, is gained. The Reign of God which he inaugurates in his ministry after his baptism can be seen in the pascal transitions from death to life in the present not only within ourselves but also in the world through social witness.

Suffering and Enlightenment

The way of Christ, the way of the cross, becomes the way of enlightenment, which is the way of resurrection. Often after a period of trial, 'hanging in there' and trusting God in the process, a person will emerge with insight and more clarity. A new level is reached in which the person is more enlightened in Christ.

The following story indicates a helpful aspect of the use of the language of light in the spiritual growth of the Christian:

> A GREATER SPIRIT IS FOUND
>
> *John had enjoyed the back-to-earth period of his life, especially his years in a rain forest of Queensland in northern Australia. As a child he had been through the Roman Catholic school system of first communion and confirmation but had left it behind. As a young adult he joined 'the Journey' in the hope of progressing along a spiritual path further, a path that he valued to date in terms of connection to nature and its beauty. He wanted to see if Christianity now could connect with him and his recent experiences. Well into the process John came to a simple awareness: "I have found a greater spirit than the spirit of the forest."*

The natural light in northern Australia is very bright much of the time. Surrounded by the richness and succulence of untamed nature you can feel a form of serenity and peace, a harmony with all things. The 'Easter Journey' process and other exposures to Christianity, however, can bring a person to see the light shining in the darker, deeper places of the human heart. This spirit is indeed bigger. The spiritual light of Christ is stronger than natural or created light.[41]

Hence at the end of the Anglican baptism service a lit candle is given to the newly baptised with the these of similar words, "you have passed from darkness to light; shine as a light to the glory of God."[42]

The 'shining' is an interior 'shining' that results from the passage from death to life taken by the baptised in this life. Once spiritual light, the light of God, accesses the darkened regions of the human heart that light will emanate forth to others and into the world around. As creatures made in the image of God the divine light must find its way into all areas of human life for our redemption to be genuine and whole. On the Mount of Transfiguration the three disciples saw that light shining from Christ. As the Russian Orthodox tradition maintains, they were bathed momentarily in it as a precursor of the resurrection light that they were to be bathed in after Easter and Pentecost.

The 'shining' spoken of here is a paradoxical phenomenon. As a reality within the Christian life it is sometimes recognisable by others but is usually unrecognised by ourselves. This is a characteristic of spiritual light. With its presence within us it is accompanied by the growth of a deeper desire for prayer, a sense of humility, clarity of understanding and a more ready compassion for others. These are qualities of which we do become aware as they emerge as the fruit of suffering through the work of the Spirit. This is why often after a period of time since an ordeal a person will get to the point of saying 'Now I would not be without that experience, as horrendous as it was at the time, for the understanding and outlook I now have.'

"Blessed are the cracked for they let the light in!" It is not only the saints in light, the light of heaven, that surround us in the great cloud of witnesses (Hebr. 12.1) – many of whom in their times were very "cracked" – but also the saints on earth, our companions on the way, who have struggled, trusted and won through, to be bathed more in the light of God.

Almighty God, whose most dear Son went not up to joy
but first he suffered pain,
and entered not into glory
before he was crucified:
mercifully grant that we,
walking the way of the cross,
may find it none other than the way
of life and peace; through Jesus Christ our Lord.
(a traditional Anglican prayer)

36 Also referred to in Chapter 1.
37 Kavanagh p.175.
38 Deriving from one of St Paul's teachings on baptism – recorded in Galatians 3:27f.: "You who were baptized into Christ have clothed yourselves with Christ: there is no longer Jew or Greek, slave or free, male and female – all are one in Christ Jesus."
39 The three fold questions on the left hand side and the corresponding responses on the right hand side are taken from the Australian Anglican order of service or Baptism in *A Prayer Book for Australia* and are the questions asked of candidates immediately prior to their baptism.
40 As we saw in Chapter 4 *eis* is a Greek word translatable as 'into'.
41 At the same time there is an important connection between the spiritual light of God in which we need to grow and a commitment to sustain the threatened environment in which natural light created by God shines. Spiritual strengthening leads to a deepened concern and alertness for environmental action in our time.
42 Words from *The Australian order of service for Baptism*, *A Prayer Book for Australia.*

SECTION III

OUT OF THE DEPTHS

Dynamics of Edge and Centre

Living our Baptism

Shared initiation journeys give rise to the discovery of particular themes that are not strong in present church culture. It is the purpose of this section to explore further some of the avenues that arise by way of the process with adults as these take place early in this century. A ready example here is to do with spiritual friendship. As we shall see in the chapter of this title (Ch.13) this topic arises out of the experience of the participant-companion relationship that develops in the process. It has a distinctive relevance for the Church of today and tomorrow.

Six avenues are explored here with a group incident presented at the start of each chapter. Each incident reveals a moment in the 'Journey' that had the potential to open up a particular theme as freshly encountered. The theme of the chapter is then explored on that basis.

Traditions of the past are tapped in these explorations in an attempt to give renewed expression to them as a part of future Christian life and witness. The themes are far from exhaustive of any future shape of Christianity. Nevertheless, as topics they highlight the giftedness of the edge-centre dynamic in the life of the Church, of the Church truly being the baptising community. The consequences of this mode of being church involves, for example, going more deeply into the Christian mystery-contemplation (Ch.12) and moving more widely in contact with others – refugee neighbours (Ch.14) – than has been customarily emphasised in the past.

CHAPTER 10

WELL OF THE WORD

Group Incident:

Alan listened to the account of the disciples sleeping in the boat and Jesus stilling the storm. He exclaimed, "I don't believe in the miraculous!" Then, pausing for reflection and challenged by the question of what struck him in the story, he found a distinct 'wake-up call' to look more deeply into his life and began to see that his life was of value in the manner of Jesus' bringing value to the disciples' lives and stilling the storm around them. (A longer description of this incident can be found in Chapter 7.)

How are we to read scripture? What has been our experience of reading scripture? Most of us have had a mixed set of experiences interpreting scripture. We have favourite passages and ones we don't like. We may have been in study groups where someone takes opportunity to interpret a passage narrowly and in so doing seems to take away some inspiration that we thought we saw in it.

Reading with the Critical Eye of the Mind

The bible has been dug around in for over the last 250 years since the Enlightenment as an investigative site. Scholars have critiqued passages to get at what may or may not have happened historically. Layers of interpretation, for example, are now recognised as residing in the Pentateuch, the first five books of the Old Testament. In accounts of the crossing of the Red (or Reed) Sea progressive versions became increasingly dramatic. Scientific scholarship has been presented as an objective hermeneutic whereby it claims that the isolated individual, namely the scholar, can uncover meaning and that meaning is determined by the scientific approach.

This kind of analysis has contributed significantly to Christians' understanding of biblical passages. And there have been reactions to it. The fundamentalist movement emphasises a literal or near-literal reading. Sadly, many of the courses of adult inquiry into Christianity are based on this view of scripture so that in practice participants are exposed to verses plucked out of context in order to make persuasive points.

We can contrast the reading of scripture in the 'Easter Journey', the African Bible Study method, with both the critical reading of text and the isolated verse, text plucking, literal approach. The African method as an intuitive approach, I am arguing, claims a priority of place in interpretation, in the listening and the sharing of response to text, for the purpose of coming to faith and growth in faith. At the same time, use can be made of both the other approaches as a secondary endeavour. Alan's story is illustrative.

In the above incident Alan accessed a deeper response to the passage at hand, having a 'wake-up call' to value his life more. This primary response was honoured and nurtured. For him, secondarily, to hear a contribution of the scholarly critical work done on the passage, was also helpful so that his heart and mind were able to progress together from this point. The scholarly contribution was to say that in all probability the passage was a story repeatedly told in the Early Church as great encouragement in a time of stormy persecution for those who had set sail within the little boat of the Church. The passage is therefore saying that, similar to the disciples in the boat, the threatened lives of Christians in following generations were of infinite value to their Master. It was of great interest to Alan, in his new mode of being, to note that the significance of the story doesn't simply lie in the acceptance of Jesus' having miraculous powers over nature. Furthermore, as Alan continued his own reflections the words that repeatedly occur in the bible, "do not be afraid" became an important mantra for him. Taking up such an isolated verse after his primary encounter with scripture was at this point appropriate.

The intuitive, reflective approach that is being emphasised in this book has had an important place historically in the life of the Church, especially before the Enlightenment, and was found in monasteries with the personal practice of the *Lectio Divina*. Now, after 250 years since the Enlightenment, there are the beginnings of a dynamic of retrieval taking place in various parts of the Church whereby this kind of approach, by individuals and in groups, is being practiced more.

As we saw in Chapter 7, by using the African method, participants respond to the text themselves and then listen to each others' responses. At times the quality of response and sharing is such that possibilities for life changes genuinely occur, as happened for Alan, with a vista opening up before him to start to value his life. Furthermore, with the method used, opportunity is given for group members to say in what way another person's response has been helpful to them. A rich fabric of responses develops such that participants begin to be built up in a communal type faith and way of believing.

Another avenue of objective-styled interpretation has arisen in recent decades from various ideological approaches to text:

liberationist, feminist, black ... as a part of these respective theologies. These approaches bring a "hermeneutic of suspicion" to the text claiming that layers of relevant interpretation have been lost due to the western (white, male) dominance of scriptural perspectives. Interpretation is pursued from the vantage point of the oppression of a particular community or section of society. When this form of interpretation is done in a grass-roots manner, by groups or communities, a close similarity is displayed between this approach and the intuitive method. What is characteristic of the similarity is attention to the needs of the vulnerable and their restoration. Later in this chapter reference is made to how the grassroots interpretations of the African method of the initiation process leads to a priority of listening to the poor and vulnerable.

Reading with the Open Eye of the Heart

We can see in the intuitive approach and in particular the African model that there is a moving beyond an objective hermeneutic to uncovering meaning through the interaction between the text (and what the author intended) and the community (the group). A plurality of interpretation is exposed as each person encounters the text. Whilst the objective approach is important for Christian understanding it is far from exhaustive of what is needed to enter into the spiritually rich and fertile domain of the bible. We can be helped by an application of the critical method but when it is used alone, it can be dry, unrelated to circumstances, even boring.

Another issue regarding use of scripture, of a grassroots kind, bears in on our discussion at this point. When inviting church members to join the 'Easter Journey', either as companions or to re-affirm their faith together with inquirers, it is often their past negative experience of bible study that has to be addressed. They need to hear: "we shall not be engaging in 'traditional bible study'." 'Traditional bible study' was largely the locally based approach used during the twentieth century. In this approach participants are asked prepared questions in relation to a passage and are informed before or after this activity as to what the text actually means. After acknowledging their alienating experiences with this kind of use of scripture inquirers often then agree to embark on a different approach.

In the intuitive model people are not invited to see behind the text; this would encourage a distancing of themselves from the text thereby deflecting attention to some form of empirical examination. When, for example, the text is put into a framework of one of the major themes of scripture (like covenant or redemption) to wrap around the text, this focus can diminish the discoveries that individuals in the reflective method are able to make.[43]

Conditions apply for the use of the reflective, interactive method. An attitude of mutual respect and listening both to oneself and others is emphasised. An approach of openness to the text is invited. Interestingly, this allows for – as in Alan's case at first – a sceptical approach to the truth of scripture in which the mind overshadows a person's genuine, heart-felt response. The respect for the text that is requested of group members amounts to approaching it in some way as sacred text. If any inquirers regard the text as "myth" (what they mean by myth at this point is non-factual, historically untrue), then respect for this "myth" is asked of the group.

Where there has been an inherited heavy feeling of moralising in association with the bible, the approach here usually enables this burden to be overcome. The bible then becomes "a conversation partner and not a club to beat ourselves with."[44] Attentive-ness to the text and the immediate human context means that participants begin to see things with fresh eyes. We can say that this reading of text is subjective and has a prior place to an objective reading. We do not mean however that the act of reading and response here, as subjective, means that it is contrived, made up or even being merely 'my opinion'. Heart response to text is not a mere opinion since opinion is a 'from the top of the head' type reaction. The response here, rather, arises from the subject, the whole subject at hand, that is, the person in response to text and the text's impact on the person. By contrast, the objective reading is given, derived from the thoughts and work of others, from their scholarship and their scholarly environment. Their findings can be helpful and are needed, as we have seen, within the whole enterprise of growth and understanding.

The kind of scriptural text that is used here is usually, but not always, that of gospel story. Scriptural story, and indeed many a good story, including those of the sacred texts of other great traditions, gets alongside the readers. Readers are then enabled to enter the story consciously or unconsciously. There is a playfulness that the structure of a good story provides, allowing for a remarkable breadth of response without losing the central focus. At the same time there is an ambiguity in stories and story telling that not only allows for this breadth of response but can take the reader beyond its constraints:

Biblical thinking and story telling have structures which provide constraints to interpretation and also enable us to perceive points at which the story breaks the bounds of these constraints.[45]

This grass-roots retrieval of the scriptures, whereby groups of people have the bible in their laps and attend to the text of scripture with personal response, would have delighted John Wesley! Amidst the malaise of the English Church in the eighteenth century it was his instigated "method" of bible studying cells that formed many people in the faith and created the base for the English evangelical revival.

We can be helped in our appreciating the many sidedness of text interpretation by mention of the image of the text *as a prism*. The intuitive method in practice can be likened to a prism through which light of interpretation from different angles shines. From where you as a participant sit you receive a particular fracture of the light. It is for you as you are and if you describe your response it can bring further light to yourself and to those who sit with you.

We saw a vivid example of this in the group reflection on the passage about the women drying Jesus' feet with her hair (Luke 7:36-50) in Chapter 7. One person's response was simply to want to sit with her own sense of wonder of how God can 'touch life'. Another person discovered a sense of unworthiness, not liking what he saw inside himself but also becoming mindful of the acceptance of Jesus. A third person looked at the warmth and compassion of Jesus in the face of the pharisee-host's objections; he was being stirred to a more compassionate life. The sharing in the group enabled further moments of grace for others present.

Continuing with the image of the prism and light shining out through it in different angles, we could say that in group reflection members start to realise that they are actually receiving spiritual light. Without romanticising the sense here, in the process of inner receiving and outer sharing, a kind of 'soft brilliance' can be gleaned. This is especially noteworthy in that often what people share has a vulnerable dimension to it, requiring help and healing. It is with the way of all human dimensions being brought to the text that we can affirm with John Calvin that scripture has the capacity truly to illuminate our understanding: it is a guide on the path. The Holy Spirit is at work in the communal gathering around the 'well of the Word', bringing light in the way of revelation to pilgrims in their circumstances.

Other intuitive readings of scripture function in a similar manner. The monastic-based discipline of *Lectio Divina* is an example. It is different however in that it is normally used on an individual, private level. The Ignatian method of imaginatively entering the story provides a slightly different structure but is basically alike.

The heart approach to scripture practiced in community has the effect of awakening, of revealing spiritual truth, of bringing avenues of healing and of conversion to the reader.

Attending to passages of scripture is always an alerting endeavour in which any one person's interpretation can change from one time to another. My response to hearing text now will probably be quite different in some months' time.

The Word in Community

The 'Easter Journey' trains people for alertness to hear what the text is saying to them now, in their present situation. This kind of alertness is activated in the two communal contexts of reading and listening to gospel passages – one, in the small group with responses shared, and, the other, in the gathered assembly of worship, especially the eucharistic liturgy when all stand and turn expectantly to hear the reading of the Gospel. In each context we are asking the question – what is Christ "clothed in his Gospel" (Calvin) saying to us today? In the first, group participants share their responses one with another in the interpersonal environment. In the second, the preacher presents interpretation for the community in order to assist in mediating the Word to all individually and communally. Both communal settings, one small, the other larger, are important; we may even say vital, for the discipleship of the Christian person and the community.

Before concluding this chapter two further aspects of scriptural interpretations need to be mentioned. The first is that not all pieces of scripture carry the same weight. To illustrate, the New Testament scholar Sandra Schneider refers to St Paul's command to women to wear veils at worship (1Cor. 11:11-16). This instruction is clearly ignored today as being of little importance, whereas looking at the passage more widely his command for unity at the Eucharist (1 Cor. 11:17-22) – is still today a matter of significance. It becomes clear in such examples that whilst a surface meaning of some specific texts may not be important or relevant in the present, a more fundamental concern may be at stake that needs attending to, as the wider dimensions of the text come into view.

Secondly, the process of group scriptural response, being grassroots situated, leads in time to active attention to the underside of the local, and maybe wider, community. As the group learns to accept the sharing of vulnerability one with another, as a wholesome, creative activity, one in which the Spirit works and heals, the group then begins to take up God's concern for the poor and vulnerable. Often a group or church community after a time in using scripture intuitively will become involved in a form of social action.[46]

In conclusion, we can ask what priority should this interpretive method have in the community of faith corporately as well as individually? If the Word of God speaks through 'Holy Writ' when approached openly and reverently in a group setting, can attending to it in all situations help and inform, check and direct the faith community? If so, is the Church corporate, local and wider, prepared to practise this? Can we apply the method more to church meetings and other gatherings in which members assemble to discuss concerns, joys and struggles?

Bonhoeffer summoned faith communities to read scripture as communities and to encounter the biblical word over against ourselves as well as for the revitalisation of ourselves; to engage in both for the purpose of discipleship. Moreover, as others have remarked, no one line of scriptural or theological emphasis should totally frame the community's self-understanding and ministry:

No single interpretative interest can guarantee the maintenance of a community of faithful people. As a community they are actively engaged in the process of ordering their lives in accordance with those texts that are related to the various situations they find themselves in.[47]

Whatever our situation holds for us we can at any time and in any place gather around the 'well of the Word' for refreshment, light, challenge and peace – for *dabah* – the Hebrew for 'word' that is only translatable in connection with 'deed' or 'act'; that is, the word of God comes to us as *event* as the scriptures portray, always to influence and change us. "My word will not return to me empty, says the Lord " (Isa. 45:23).

43 See Fowl and Jones, *Reading in Communion and Engaging Scripture* for some further considerations.

44 A quote from an unpublished essay, by Paul Dalzell, *Scriptural Hermaneutics and the Making of Christians*, 2003.

45 John Goldingay, *Models for Interpretation of Scripture Eerdmans*, 1995, p.77.

46 See the writings of South African theologian Gerrud West on grassroots biblical interpretation that focuses on this point.

47 S.E. Fowl and L.G.Jones, *Reading in Communion*, Wipf & Stock 1998 p.20.

CHAPTER 11

WHAT ON EARTH IS SIN?

Group Incident

A young woman was taken aback by the mention of sin. Her defences rose as she expressed her irritation of the frequent reference to sin in her previous involvement with the Church. "Are we really as guilty as that? ... Isn't there too much grovelling before God?"

True and False Sense of Sin

In Australian 'Easter Journey' groups a negative effect of Sunday School days lingers with some participants. What remains with them is a sense of a judgmental, remote God, a divine figure who frowns upon them. This image engenders a false sense of sin. Maybe the longer-term legacy of the past in terms of Australian history plays a part in this unfortunate pre-occupation.

There is a difference in the religious legacies of the New World when we compare the settlements of North America and Australia. The orientation that the immigrants to the American colonies carried was one of religious trust and freedom. The new-comers to the great south land two centuries later arrived with quite different spiritual influences and perceptions. Initially, as a penal colony, Church and State worked hand in hand to administer the law among a predominantly convict population. Epitomising this predicament, the Rev'd Samuel Marsden, rode around on his horse as both priest and magistrate, dealing out punishments. As free settlers also arrived a heavy moralising character regarding religion continued to dominate.[48]

It is not too far fetched to detect cultural traces of the unhealthy legacy of a judging God passed down through the generations within Australian culture. Harshness of land and harshness of history have worked hand in hand. The image of a judging God is of One without active compassion and whose attention is on wrong doing: "if possible", the immigrant to the Great South Land surmises, "this is God to be ignored rather than possibly trusted."

The young woman quoted at the start at this chapter progressed to see a different picture of Jesus and his God in the gospels. She perceived the acceptance and healing dimension that the process opens up through the gospel encounter exercise. The ministry of the process could be described as a gathering up of ourselves in God's grace wherein the negative forces in our lives, including our culpability, begin to be transformed. As participants continue to come together in the group attention is not primarily given to our culpability, just as Jesus did not normally draw attention to people's culpability in his ministry of healing and forgiveness.[49] Healing and forgiveness are accessed before any response of personal confession of culpability may take place. Following Jesus' approach enables people to sort out what is false and what is true culpability or sin.

Sin and Evil

Our difficulty in talking about sin is that there is a mix of sin and evil. These two elements are in a state of interaction within the human condition. How sin and evil interact is best portrayed in story. I offer two such stories.

In the film *Walk the Line* the singer Johnny Cash returns home ...

STRUGGLE WITH THE PRESENT AND THE PAST

After a hectic few weeks of being on the road, performing at concerts in various towns, late nights and the ready availability of alcohol and drugs assail him. Returning home to his family, arriving exhausted and stressed, he gets into a fight with his wife and finds himself attacking her, pinning her to the floor, as the children peep through the doorway.

Cash's childhood was difficult. His father is seen repeatedly belittling him. At the death of his older brother with whom he had a close relationship, the young Johnny is left isolated and made to feel guilty by his father for the accident that caused his brother's death.

The negative forces experienced in his childhood inevitably are carried through into Cash's adult life. They play their part as deep-seated emotional elements in the event portrayed on his return home from being on the road. His attack on his wife is an action that cannot be excused – he must take responsibility for what he has done. What however must come into focus in taking responsibility for himself and his behaviour, are the immediate and past influences on his life, namely, the trials and temptations of the road show environment, and also his low self-esteem that derives from the severe lack of his father's encouragement in his early days. Finding a way forward is a tall order, as the film powerfully portrays.

The second story pictures the anchorite Julian of Norwich, in the fourteen century, living a life devoted to prayer in a wall cell of a church in what was a large city at that time …

WINDOW ONTO THE WORLD

One window looked into the church and another onto the street below through which townsfolk could speak to her. She lived at

> *a time of great poverty and suffering in England largely precipitated by the plague. One day a passer-by stopped and asked her, "Where can we find sin?" Her reply was to say, "I only see the ravages of sin."*

Julian's reply was based on her own spiritual outlook on the world and the soul, an outlook that saw the love of God as all-embracing. Her words reflect an understanding that the causes of situations of destructiveness ("ravages") are various and are to be seen as a mixture of inherited evils including natural forces, such as disease and individual wrong-doing in the present. The human wilfulness of sin, according to Julian's view, as the only action that causes a bad situation, is nearly impossible to find as an isolated phenomenon.

This understanding of sin in the situation of her day opens up the need for we humans to see ourselves as sinners in solidarity with each other, helping each other get out of the mires we find ourselves. The idea of sinner solidarity is non-judgmental and presumes that 'I may have done the same kind of thing as you have done if I had been in the particularities of your circumstances'. After his personal crisis Johnny Cash marries June, his singing partner on stage. She becomes such a solidarity person, a true companion, and assists him to overcome his mire in a way he could not have done alone.

The Scope of Redemption

Why then have we in the twentieth and early twenty-first century Church got ourselves into the predicament of a view of sin that is overly narrow and doesn't acknowledge the mix with evil? And in addition we can ask, why do we not concentrate our focus on the remedy for sin and evil, that is, the sweep of the healing love of God in the event of Jesus Christ?

The answer in broad terms is that from the medieval period

the western Church has preached a dominant theology of personal sin and guilt with the accompanying need for its redemption. This approach has been at the expense of a wider, more liberating perspective.

In Acts 3 Peter puts the 'mixed case' for the causes of the death of Jesus, not laying the blame solely at the feet of the people whom he addresses:

You handed over and rejected the Holy and Righteous One … You killed the Author of life … And now my friends, I know that you acted in ignorance, as also did our rulers. In this way God fulfilled what was foretold through the prophets (v.14-17).

With these words Peter emphasises the plan of God's redemption as the grounds of appeal for repentance of sins and changed lives. Communal culpability is only the secondary reason for the need to repent. He indicates that the people, including the rulers, were caught up in the collusion of inherited and collective negative forces – "you acted in ignorance." Yet he also names their culpability: "you handed (him) over." The main issue at stake in the situation is for the people to turn to God and in giving up the negatives of the past to respond to the proclamation and presence of the love of God poured out in Jesus.

Regarding the legacy of the western church we are discussing here, a modern classic that helps with this issue is John Hick's *Evil and the Love of God*. Hicks outlines that in the third century the theologian Iranaeus was foremost in moulding the thinking of the Church on the subject of sin and evil. Looking at the original state of humanity as depicted in the Bible Iranaeus pictures Adam and Eve in the Garden as children. Their sin is "accordingly not presented as damnable revolt but rather as calling forth God's compassion on account of their weakness and vulnerability … Within God's providence man is being taught by his contrasting experience of good and evil to value the one and shun the other. Hence there exists the mixture of good and evil in our world."[50] Hick cites a quote of N. P. Williams to sum up this foundational Christian thinking:

Our study of the … Church of the late second century reveals an interpretation of the Fall doctrine which, whilst preserving the essential outlines of Pauline teaching, wears a humane, reasonable and curiously modern complexion … It gives a picture of primitive man as frail, imperfect and child-like – a picture which on the whole … is by no means incapable of harmonisation with modern science today. It exaggerates neither the height from which, nor the depth to which, the first humans are alleged to have fallen. It finds in the inherited disorder of our nature rather a weakness to be pitied than an offence to be condemned.[51]

This line of thinking in no way is intended to veil our eyes from the horrors as well as the daily realities in which we can see a high level of human culpability in evil situations. The Eastern Orthodox Church which has maintained the witness of the thinking presented here through the centuries, places in its discipline a strong emphasis on personal confession and absolution.

My own involvement for several years now with the Karen people of Burma in their oppression by the government military provides me with a daily reminder of the fact of human culpability. There is the near silence of the western media over what in effect is a form of ethnic cleansing similar to the horrors of the war in Bosnia in the 1990s. During sermons on mission partnership in Australian parishes I can only mention the fact of the unspeakable victimisation of men, women and children: the details would be too much to bear for most church-goers.

I have sought to present an integrated perspective on the subject of sin and evil in this chapter. It stands as a picture of the human condition that better fits reality and enables us to have a truer biblical vision of redemption in Christ, rather than the narrow perspective that has been handed down to us in much of our church traditions. Fortunately, many of the recent expressions of liturgical worship in our main-stream churches are regaining much of this perspective.

Such a vision frees the Church's outlook from a fixation on law and morality. It holds the capacity to attract the seeker. It places the Jesus of the Gospels as the agent of freedom in the centre and looks to the New Order of God's Reign with its signs in the present and its promise of fulfilment to come:

We know that the whole creation has been in labour pains until now … and we ourselves who have the first fruits of the Spirit, groan inwardly while we wait for adoption, the redemption of our bodies. (Rom. 8:23).

48 The social character of the early days of Australian settlement has been highlighted in recent decades by such publications of *The Fatal Shore* by Robert Hugh (1987) and *The Commonwealth of Thieves* by Thomas Kenneally (2006).

49 It was only to the Pharisees that he directed attention to (their) culpability.

50 John Hick, Fontana 1970 p.222.

51 Hick pp.222-23.

CHAPTER 12

ACCESSIBLE CONTEMPLATION

Group Incident:
It was only the second meeting. The leader decided to end the session with a period of silence with the group seated around a lit candle. In no time at all there was an atmosphere of stillness – it was like ducks to water! … Some of the inquirers commented afterwards that they valued the silence although it was new to them.

Many people find contemplative prayer difficult to access. The short silence in the group session was at least a start. The comment that followed was a reminder that there is a great thirst in western culture for silence in the form of contemplation, despite the impression of it seeming to be difficult.

Searching
My own journey with contemplation has been one of delayed discovery.

> ICY BEGINNINGS
>
> *From a young age I wanted to learn the way of contemplative prayer. When I was at theological college in Scotland the student body was encouraged to attend a daily half-hour meditation at seven in the morning. It was usually dark at that*

> *hour and very cold. Some students wandered into the gloom of the chapel in their cassocks; others were clad with additional large, black cloaks. Their attire contributed to the gloom. No-one had given me instruction in methods of meditation so I used to sit or kneel in my place thinking that I must pray in my mind or try and ponder religious things. It was always quite a struggle. As I look back on the time I imagine icy drops of water trickling down the bluestone walls! I somehow knew that what I was doing was not contemplative prayer. I envied a couple of fellow students who sat very still and seemed absorbed in something that seemed spiritual for the length of time …*

It wasn't until thirty years later that I was able truly to access meditation when I attended a week long retreat in Sydney with Laurence Freeman, Director of the World Community for Christian Meditation (WCCM). During those many preceding years I had certainly practised styles of meditation of the guided prayer type with silence – a form of prayerful stillness that engages the mind and our thinking. But here at last was access to the deeper, great Christian tradition of contemplation.

Following the school of John Main and the tradition of the mantra may not be the only way into the field but, as an available avenue, it certainly provides the route for many. At the retreat there were 250 people; only three were clergy. WCCM is a growing large movement of mainly lay people who meet in cells weekly for meditation in many countries around the world.

The Dalai Lama in his visits to the West often encourages his listeners to search out the paths of meditation and contemplation in their own religious traditions. Many young people in our culture sadly think that these paths do not exist in the western Christian tradition. 'You go to the East for that'. Their ignorance is understandable since, as my own experience tells me, Christian practice is not easily made available. In our churches the orientation towards activism – the emphasis on doing – is mainly what they have seen.

In this chapter I shall trace what Christian contemplation is, as I see its accessibility in the West. My perceptions are largely influenced by the teachings of Laurence Freeman. The contemplative path is a part of the rich tradition of Christian mysticism from *The Cloud of Unknowing* to St John of the Cross and into the present. I shall briefly trace this broader tradition. As people participate in the 'Easter Journey', the reflective process and the openness to spiritual experience gears them for an interest and entry into this great tradition. Equally, many inside and outside the Church are thirsting for these depths of living water.

Finding

Contemplative prayer is one of the spokes of the wheel of Christian prayer along with other forms – worship, intercession, confession, praying with scripture ... with the hub of the wheel being the mind of Christ. Contemplative prayer is the form of prayer that invites us to go beyond our thought and therefore beyond the ego. Emptying the mind by use of the mantra, or possibly some other approach, is a way to be in the presence of God. As Fr John Main once wrote:

We are invited to unlock the shackles of limitation, to be freed from being prisoners within our own self-limiting egos. Conversion is just this liberation and expansion arising when we turn from ourselves to the infinite God.[52]

At the same time contemplation is not an easy road into some form of spiritual excitement. As Laurence Freeman[53] says of contemplation, it is an escape from fantasies into reality, a penetration into the deeper levels of reality that is quite ordinary; we often expect the extraordinary to happen; if it does, ignore it. The task is to slow down into who we are, the real, what is present ... out of our heads into a more inclusive contact.

This form of prayer practices silence. "There is nothing so much like God as silence." (Meister Eckhart). Growing a love of silence is the gradual realisation of this mystical truth. Silence is not the absence of noise, but the absence of thought. Meditation is the work of silence. In meditation we choose, as inevitably the mind wanders, to come back to the centre repeatedly. The repetition of the mantra (*Marantha* – Come, Lord, come – or some other phrases like *Lord have mercy, Abba, Jesus* …) involves us in not thinking about the mantra but simply and slowly saying it.

I like the teaching about the ever present matter of distraction. That is, gently to return again and again to the mantra. Distraction is like having wandered off the path into the forest. All we need do is come back continually to the path.

The tradition teaches that connection with stillness is where God arises and is simultaneously a way to self-knowledge on a deep level. Accepting the notion of 'God arising' does not mean that we will have holy thoughts at points in the times of meditation or even that should aim to have them. In the process of slowing down in meditation we go down into the inner chamber of the heart. We may not have visited this space since childhood or only in a fleeting visit during a crisis. In time we discover it is the place where truly home is.

Moving into contemplative prayer is not into 'my prayer' but the prayer of Jesus (John Main). All we do is allow Jesus to act in our souls. It is an act of non-controlling trust, a challenge to ego desire. We are invited into this way of praying alongside the reading of scripture, participating in the Eucharist and engaging in personal mental prayer. It is about abandoning the ego to God and staying in the discipline of a daily set-aside time.

Its rooted-ness is in the teaching of Jesus where he continually points to the need for an inner orientation towards God and a corresponding self-knowledge. In the Sermon on the Mount we find the foundations for contemplative prayer:

interiority and silence before God – "shut the door" – go into your heart and be there before God
stay in the present, the 'Now' – "do not worry about tomorrow"
attention or mindfulness – "set your minds on the Kingdom".

Walking the Path

Meditation develops contentment. It engenders clarity of mind and insight in daily life. It puts us in touch with the state inherent in our being which is the Kingdom within. At the same time there is an undulating path to tread.

The desert fathers and mothers of the fourth century began to develop the tradition. With the establishing of Christianity in the Empire they went to the wilds of the Egyptian desert and to other remote places for fear that the Faith would become compromised. They devoted themselves to this way of prayer. Soon they found themselves confronted with *acedia*, the feeling of discouragement, hopelessness, loss and disconnection that comes from walking this spiritual path. In their community life the predicament was named for what it is and emphasis was laid upon gentle perseverance (returning to your cell) together with the counsel and encouragement of an elder.

The commentator of the life of the desert communities, John Cassian, in his *Conferences*, writes about the spiritual dynamics and processes of these courageous souls. He mentions the use of the mantra. At one point he describes what he calls the *pax perniciosa* – a lethal sleep – an evading of the work of solitude, not actually seeking God, but seeking an experience of respite and rest, an escape from the present situation. This is the ego in the driver's seat ... it's scary not to have a driver.

Various forms of help can be given to the contemporary meditator. Think of the road to Emmaus account in Luke's gospel. Arriving at the village Christ disappears at the breaking of the bread but this doesn't mean he is not still present. In meditation we come to the "place of calm abiding" (a Buddhist phrase) but then after a time many people stop meditating. The solution to our impatience is gently to persevere in the paradox of the contemplative journey being our work and yet all God's work. A great encouragement is to belong to a weekly or fortnightly meditation group. Then there are the modern writers of books to read in the field, such as Thomas Merton, Morton Kelsey and Rowan Williams, each of whom can encourage us.

The Mystical Life

The most famous classic piece of literature of English background on contemplation is *The Cloud of Unknowing* by an anonymous author of the fourteenth century. Fundamental to the teaching of this book is that the person new to prayer needs to proceed by love and not knowledge. The author contrasts knowing power and loving power:

"To the knowing power God is evermore incomprehensible, but to the loving power he is, in every man diversely, all comprehensible to the full ... for why, love may reach to God in this life but not knowing.[54]

On this path the soul embarks upon a state of unknowing which is named as a kind of darkness:

From the beginning it is usual to feel nothing but a kind of darkness around the mind, as it were, a cloud of unknowing ... this darkness and cloud will remain between you and your God. You will feel frustrated (but) ... your heart will not relinquish the delight of his love. Learn to be at home in the darkness.[55]

The darkness is described as a way of ignorance and this is an inner way which the pilgrim of prayer is to expect:

So the via amoris, the way of love, has to be preceded by a via negativa, a way of ignorance; the negative dimension that makes possible the blind stirring of darkness is a lack of knowing.[56]

Then, in the seventeenth century, St John of the Cross teaches that the darkness is in reality the light of God as received by finite human persons. The light blinds the soul, and is dark night – a night of faith. "The spiritual theology of John begins with the belief that all human beings are rooted in God's love. To live in awareness of this reality is a sign of what he terms 'the great awakening'. "To live with oneself as central is a sign of illusion", he writes in the *Living Flame of Love* (Ch.4).[57]

The dark night for John is the process of disillusionment or shedding illusions. Detachment is therefore necessary. The dark night of the senses is a detachment from pleasure, that is, from one's own concern for self. Detachment is always a part of the experience of transforming love. John's teaching could be summed as:

Our prayer is more God's work in me and not my work … In a further movement of stripping, this progress inwards towards God brings a new sense of peace and also deeper awareness of sin. There is a healing process. Our ego centred-ness collapses. "And through the integration of conscious and unconscious, light and dark, head and heart, we come to knowledge of ourselves for the first time at a wonderful, mysterious level … as sinners who are loved.[58]

Thomas Merton in the mid twentieth century wrote extensively about contemplation. Referring to much that is dissatisfactory in modern life he wrote;

The greatest need of our time is to clean out the enormous mass of mental and emotional rubbish that clusters our minds … Without this housecleaning we cannot begin to see. Unless we see, we cannot begin to think.[59]

The seeing and thinking Merton refers to are the required new beginnings of contemplative prayer. He also makes a point to address the danger of domesticating God in our times and of the importance of the mystery of God that is at the heart of this tradition.

The Anglican monk and theologian Harry Williams writes of spiritual growth with a psychological interpretation of inner darkness:

The process of self-knowledge is a journey through uncomfortable regions. To arrive at my truest self where God dwells it is necessary for me to pass through some pretty ugly country. To find the God within me I have on the way to encounter aspects of myself from which I tend to run away and hide ... I have to learn to love these aspects. This involves considerable turmoil. Then I shall find God within me ... the love, joy and peace which is my truest self ...[60]

The American spiritual writer Alan Jones comments that depth psychology has helped the modern person of prayer enter the realm of darkness and formlessness creatively.

The quotes in the last section of this chapter, as brief as they are, indicate that there is a magnificently rich field in the Christian mystical tradition that is available for the practice of contemplative prayer. The signposts of the pilgrimage are geared for inner transformation, for enlightenment, as participants in the 'Easter Journey' find. Inaugurated at baptism, the pathway of prayer and spiritual life is a movement, to use a form of classical language, from the image to the likeness of Christ within us.

Twenty minutes at break of day
Ever to deepen you on the way
And then come what may
Again at close of day.

52 *Word made Flesh*, Dartman, Longman & Todd 1993, p.20.
53 Some of my thoughts here are based on parts of Fr Laurence Freeman's addresses at the retreat in Sydney, 2005.
54 *The Cloud of Unknowing*, Chapter 1
55 *The Cloud of Unknowing*, Chapter 3
56 *The Cloud of Unknowing*, Chapter 3
57 Cited in Kenneth Leech, *True God*, Sheldon 1985 p.183.
58 Leech p.185.
59 *Conjectures of a Guilty Bystander*, Doubleday 1966 p.64.
60 *Becoming What I Am*, DLT 1977 p.86.

CHAPTER 13

SPIRITUAL FRIENDSHIP

Group Incident:

Bob, a young man, and Greg a retired, older man were companions to each other in the 'Easter Journey' group. One afternoon the two of them met for coffee. The gospel encounter in the last group session had touched something raw in Bob's life. He began to discuss the session and by means of Greg's quiet, attentive listening he was able to talk for the first time about an emotional wound from his earlier years. A trusting friendship developed that has continued since.

Many people are familiar with the reference to the special friendship between David and Jonathan, the son of Saul, in the Old Testament. The closeness of the friendship is most powerfully indicated at the time of the death of Jonathan when David exclaims:

I grieve for you, Jonathan, my brother; you were very dear to me. Your love for me was wonderful, more wonderful than that of a woman. (2 Sam.1:26)

Some questions readily arise from this text. Since David was a known womaniser, does this utterance disclose a blinkered view of women preventing him from entering into the mutual respect that is the ground for the growth of deep, trusting friendship between the sexes, especially within marriage? Despite this possibility, is this verse nevertheless indicative of the capacity of deep, spiritual friendship between two people of any sex and generation?

The group incident that introduces this chapter alludes to this capacity. Indeed the text, taken 'at its best', points to the extraordinary depths that can grow between two people in the area of what we are calling 'spiritual friendship'.

Until recently there has been a fear among men in western culture to spend time and develop trust on deeper levels with each other. Many a man says that his best friend is his wife. This is good, yet in another sense it is a reflection of a sad phenomenon, namely, that some men are unable to develop close relationships with other men. The emergence of men's groups in recent decades has greatly encouraged the growth of trust and deeper levels of friendship between males, as women have enjoyed among themselves for generations.

What is at the heart of spiritual friendship? What is its importance for the Christian community? As the Bob-Greg incident indicates it is about the finding of space between two people that enables a deeper sharing of life one with the other, an open trust that verges on unconditional love. Certainly for many who become involved in the 'Easter Journey', levels of friendship are experienced that are spiritually based. 'Spiritual' in the Christian sense refers here to being in the milieu or context of unconditional love which is the quality of love that God has for us humans. As we shall see this graced experience is not some perfected state: it carries its own problems, yet it is frequently revered as a gift by those who experience it. As we shall also see it needs to be viewed as an integral part of Christian community life as these communities find their way into an increasingly uncertain and possibly hostile future.

Any discussion of spiritual friendship is difficult to put

boundaries around in terms of where it is to be found. Firstly, we can say that it belongs to the vocation of marriage. A prayer from one order of service[61] for marriage placed immediately before the bride and the groom share their vows includes the word: "may their love for each other ever more grow to be a true reflection of your love for us all ... " This is a reference again to the divinely based quality of unconditional love. Loving friendship in marriage can look remarkably different from one couple to another and the pathway with regard to the unconditional quality of love is indeed particular to the individuals involved. We might say that this vocation is both precious and difficult in today's western world.

Friendship and affection, pre-eminently expressed between any two people, can also be present in households, between households and for that matter in small groups. The topic of spiritual friendship in the Christian domain therefore raises a fascinating set of issues to which we shall now turn. We shall briefly explore the following:

- group friendship
- the activated shadow
- heavenly friends
- the divine presence in deep friendship
- the place of this gift in the Christian community.

Group Friendship

Alcoholics Anonymous provides probably the most well-known avenue of trust, confidentiality and acceptance of small group life in the western world. Each group member can truly be 'who I am' in the intimate environment that adheres to the AA principles and meeting rules. This we could call 'group spiritual friendship'. I was interested recently to come across a book that is concerned about recovering Christian conversation in small groups.[62] According to the author the facilitator's role is to be one who models good listening for the rest of the group and maintains an awareness of the importance of non-verbal communication in the group setting.

The group experience of AA is similar to that of the 'Easter Journey' in that there is the ability in both models as caring group processes to unlock the treasure of personal discovery and revelation. With regard to the quality of group life within a Christian context the book makes the following points:

- lack of certainty is a vital ingredient for our growth as adult Christians
- there is a connection between searching and finding
- everyone has something of value to bring to the conversation about life and faith
- revelation is found in events (both shared in the group and as events in the group) which are more than words
- at times effort is required for some to see the valuable attitudes of another
- the God we worship is expressed in terms of relationships
- some young people demonstrate faith well beyond their years.

Group spiritual friendship may only last a time yet it can carry qualities of unconditional love. Two people, for example, who spoke to each other over a few group sessions and brought each other special gifts in their shared conversation, may never see each other again. On the other hand a special deep friendship may continue between them. The quality of friendship that emerges in this environment enhances personal and spiritual conversion and growth. It clearly will be of precious value for the future life of the Church.

The Activated Shadow

It is quite devastating when a confidence is betrayed either in a group setting of trust or between close, confiding friends. Such betrayal is usually a result of a non-recognition of the shadow side of human nature. The shadow often displays its wares as friends go deeper into the territory of relating and sharing. Surprising dark feelings can erupt in this mutual, inward journey. St Aelred, a 12th century monk, who had a strong interest in spiritual friendship, wrote, "we should not make close friends unless we want to walk in their shadow and to see them walk in ours."

Our shadow is the disowned or unrecognised parts of ourselves. In friendship often the other person will see aspects of it that we don't see ourselves. At the same time the shadow tends to manifest itself at first through 'my not liking something I see in the other person'. This reaction actually is more about something in myself I don't like than about the other person. The handling of the issues at stake takes care, patience and heaps of acceptance of oneself and the other person. It is true therefore to say that friendship at depth can only grow through the hardships that are exposed to it.

The relationship between Jesus and Judas can be salient at this point. The Greek novelist Nikos Kazantzakis explores their friendship in *The Last Temptation of Christ* and whilst there is no direct evidence for much of the story-line he presents it nevertheless provides a plausible portrayal of the two men's friendship in their younger years. Kazantzakis sees Jesus and Judas growing up together in the countryside of Galilee where the boys regularly saw the crucifixion by the Roman soldiers of fellow Galileans as rebels. A bond develops between them as they both see themselves wanting to respond to God's call in relation to the plight of their people. The novel pictures them travelling together to a Jewish monastery on the other side of the Jordan to seek advice from the abbot of the community.

Turning to the gospel accounts of the Last Supper we find a scene in which there is the continuance of friendship between them but with the entrance of its dark side. The disciple John lies on the Lord's breast while Judas dips his bread in the dish of betrayal. That same night Peter denies Jesus. After the supper John stays with Jesus through to the moment of his death on Calvary while Judas, afflicted with guilt, goes and hangs himself after his betraying kiss. Despite his denial Peter is restored to friendship with Jesus in the risen life.

The costliness of strong unresolved emotions is exposed in the person of Judas and his action. They emerge and play themselves out in the context of what had been a trusting friendship. The shadows of the night belong not just to the evening with the flickering lights but they also belong to the human heart and its intense impulses; its own shadows that have the potential to come to the fore dramatically and dangerously. Something in Judas, it appears, cannot tolerate in himself the non-violent stand that Jesus takes in the pending confrontation with the authorities. The inner shadows are exposed. "And it was night", John writes in his Gospel at least a couple of times during the description of these events, symbolically reflecting in these words the gravity of what is being revealed in human nature of our capacities, positive and negative, of loyalty and its opposite, in our relationships one with another.

There is a sense in which "being in friendship is to risk one's life; indeed, to lay down one's life" as Laurence Freeman writes.[63] What we find is that the territory of friendship at depth requires maturity on our part as well as a generous spirit. When two people have landed themselves in the gift of this friendship the hard work begins and the rewards are plentiful along with the dark corners that need to be worked through.

Heavenly Friends

We need the encouragement of the saints, those who have gone before us. In a certain manner they are spiritual friends to us. As soon as he was elected Pope Benedict XVI made the public comment, "Mary will help us on our journey." I warmed to the comment and at the same time was a little surprised by it. Here was this cardinal, renowned for his conservativism, now elected to lead the Roman Catholic Church, not referring to Mary in a high, formalised, doctrinal manner as Maria Immaculata or Regina Caeli or the like, but to the earthly woman, the figure of history who gave birth to the Saviour and journeyed with her son as his first disciple.

There have been encyclicals of recent decades that have re-pitched much of the understanding of Mary for the Church in more biblical terms. Here was an instance in Benedict's remark, accessible in its simplicity and tenderness as he addressed the world.

Non Roman Catholic Christians are increasingly becoming more at home with the inclusion of the mother of Jesus in the area of spirituality. There is far less anti-Catholic posturing about Mariology than there was decades ago. Many Christians – of most denominations – are beginning to consider that the witness of Mary in the Church brings a femininity of both a strong and contemplative form, that she is a great companion to us on the Christian walk.[64]

I recall an incident in an 'Easter Journey' group in which the group leader ran a session with the dual title, "Peter, warts and all – Rocky".

WARTS AND ALL DISCIPLE

The leader portrayed the disciple as his story comes to us in the gospels – his impulses and misunderstandings, his struggles, his

> *courage, his denial of Jesus and restoration. The character sketch enabled the group members not only to view him as a down-to-earth and authentic human being but also to feel that he as a disciple walks in solidarity with them in their struggles and stumblings to follow Christ. Peter – Cephas in Greek – means "rock"; it is on the rock of Peter's faith that Christ says he will build his church (Matt.16:18). After a while the group began to realise that this is what the purpose of the gospels is largely for: to encourage and enable us in the whole endeavour of discipleship. It is Christ who calls, restores, leads and enables us with all our warts, on the rocky way, as he did with Peter. At the same time we are encouraged by the closeness of Rocky's life and example.*

The Communion of Saints hence becomes a colourful tapestry of solidarity and support. In some churches the rite of baptism at Easter begins with a litany of the saints. Indeed we may say that the whole of heaven gathers around on this day. The litany brings together the faith and courage of our forebears in the family of the Faith, as spiritual friends who have gone before us. The prayer, often sung, may proceed with these or similar words:

> *Mary, mother of the Lord, pray for us.*
> *Apostles Peter and Paul, …*
> (other saints are mentioned, including possibly
> national and local)

"God is Friendship"

A discussion about the effect of the human shadow upon deep friendship can raise the question of whether such a relational enterprise is worthwhile. Could I bring damage to the other person? Will I be seriously harmed? … Is it better when all things are considered to adhere to the words of Simon and Garfunkel's song, "I am a rock. I am an island … a rock feels no pain and an island never cries ... " At this point the notion of awareness is important to name. Friendship that proceeds with the awareness that the shadow is there, present, in each of us, the content of which, known or unknown, holds the beginning of a mature approach. At the same time love of self needs to go hand in hand with this awareness. Laurence Freeman writes in a chapter on friendship:

Partnerships in such friendships will have learned to love themselves and so be capable of entrusting their most private selves to each other in full confidence.[65]

The path becomes a gifted necessity in fact for those who wish to pursue and grow in the spiritual life. The story is told of a disciple who asked the Buddha, "is spiritual friendship 50% of what's needed for the journey. The Buddha replied 100%.

The fruit that is found is not only about a high degree of personal acceptance but an emergence of more clarity in one's life, more honesty as well as hopefulness for oneself and the other:

Every relationship is a way of seeing. Spiritual friendship is a way of seeing truthfully and clearly.[66]

Furthermore, an outward energy comes into being as each person is kindled at depth and begins to envisage life and its possibilities. Freeman goes so far as to say:

We may find a way forward through the confusion of modern culture by seeing friendship in more than the perspective offered by ego-based psychology. Perhaps in friendship we can find the key for a unified and unifying moral vision which has been so disastrously shattered.[67]

Spiritually, then, the friendships of which we speak, have their basis in the friendship of Jesus. He has taken us to the Father with acceptance and love. Our spiritual friendships reflect and participate in this central truth. No darkness even of the activated shadow is devoid of the divine loving presence. The moments of deep acceptance of each person for the other through the territory of shadows, powerfully, subtly and maybe uniquely, reveal this loving presence. St Aelred explored the topic in his work, *De Amicitia Spirtiuale*. Whilst he was a realist about this path he chose to name the gift and the heart of it as "God is Friendship", as a way of saying that on this path we can discern the beauty of God's grace as deeply as it is possible this side of the grave.

Members of the Witnessing Community

We can suspect that during the early centuries of the Church's history in the face of adversity, spiritual friendships were common and strong. For example, in the record of the martyrdom of Ss Perpetua and Felicity we can read about how tenderly they supported each other. In a later century we see Ss Francis and Clare sharing a bond of prayerful support amidst the arduousness of the caring work each with their communities were doing.

Dietrich Bonhoeffer writes of the close fellowship of the student community he established at Finkenwalde in southern Germany in the 1930s. The discerning of the way forward for his church in the context of the looming dark clouds of totalitarianism meant for him a commitment to reading the scriptures together, to shared silence and to confessing their sins to one another, abiding in a *communio sanctorum*.

Spiritual friendship carries a further quality not yet mentioned in this chapter. Despite its apparent exclusivity in the Christian community to which the two persons belong – characterised by closeness and confidences shared between them – it is in fact enabling of inclusivity. Living in community requires coming to terms with one's shadow in order for the community to function well. A person can often gain a working knowledge of his or her dark, difficult side in a trusting friendship and thereby become a more effective, sharing member of the community. In this way the community that adheres to this understanding and practices it, thereby witnesses to the depth and preciousness of human life in the face of negative forces (e.g. utilitarian or totalitarian dominance).

We therefore come to realise that there is a connection between spiritual friendship and Christian witness. This connection is vital in unjust or hostile social environments. Maybe this is what is meant above in Laurence Freeman's quotation about the capacity of friendship to evoke a unified and unifying vision of society. Spiritual friendship not only is the means of support for one another in the times of political trial but presents itself as a key to moving forward together in faithful witness in the context of society's injustices.

61 Marriage Service, second form, *An Australian Prayer Book*, 1978.

62 Mark Davis, *Walking on the Shore*, A *Way of Sharing Faith in Groups*, Matthew James Publication, 2002.

63 *Common Ground, Letters to A World Community of Meditators*, Continuum International Group, 1999, p.79.

64 See the Anglican Roman Catholic International Commission (ACIC) document on Mary, 2005.

65 *Common Ground*, p.78.

66 *Common Ground*, p.76.

67 *Common Ground*, p.76.

CHAPTER 14

REFUGEE NEIGHBOURS

Group incident:

Two women in a 'Journey' group gained a special bond: one was an elderly Australian woman who had suffered considerably in her life and the other was a new refugee having recently arrived from Burma; she only spoke a little English. With the help of her husband's translation she was able to participate in the group. Yet without the need to communicate very much in words the women developed a close understanding and rapport between each other. Their hug was long and tender each Sunday morning.

Home and Horrors of War

As westerners we don't often detect the ambivalence that is in the minds of the newly arrived refugee. They are determined to express their appreciation to us for having a safe place to resettle. But clearly their hearts are elsewhere: back home. A Middle Eastern refugee has written theses lines:

> *Homes don't travel*
> *people hang onto their homes*
> *like snails to their shells.*
> *When people have to leave*
> *their homes, there remains a*
> *scar at the very place where*

people and walls meet so closely.

(Said Farhen)

For refugees, 'home' is of course literally their home. As they flee, they carry away with them in their hearts memories, bonds, loyalties and precious customs. 'Home' also carries with it the recollection of recent events, of disruption, of shock, of violence and even of the unspeakable. There are the horrible events which linger in the back of their minds, from which there is presently no escape. Only through giving substantial expression to these hurts can healing occur. At the same time, escaping from the affliction of their homeland involves an unending longing to return home.

Many local churches in Australia as well as in other countries of the western world are finding they have some refugees in their midst. Often in our church communities we have little appreciation of what these refugees have been through and what 'home' means for them. The following story exemplifies this point. It happened on a Sunday morning in the parish I was serving in.

COPING WITH THE UNSPEAKABLE

Just before the Eucharist was to begin the Karen community leader arrived to tell me some recent news. (The Karen people are one of the larger ethnic nationalities of Burma.) One of the members of the congregation, a Karen woman and mother, had learnt the night before that her village in the east of Burma had been attacked again by the government military. Her sister was a victim of the attack and had her eyes gouged out. In church I noted the woman as she sat quietly through the service that morning with no show of emotion – the Asian way. In the prayer of intercession I alluded to the Karen people's civil war, waged for 50+ years, but with no mention of the tortured woman who was so much on my mind. How could reference be made to the

> *actualities of such horrors of war in this context of worship in suburban Australia? I thought to myself. Maybe they should be, in order to catapult us out of the cocoon of our isolation and protection. Here was the victim's sister who needed caring for. She was in our midst and one of us. Yet that day I hid behind a veil of cultural and ecclesiastical respectability ...*

The phenomenon of 'refugee neighbours' is here to stay, whether we are side by side with refugees in our congregations or in our streets, schools or workplaces, or in our living rooms where, by means of the persistent reporting of world events, we are exposed to aspects of the fact of the twenty million[68] around the world who are expelled from their homes. Our long-held cocoon is collapsing. Attending to this thought I composed these lines:

> *... the neighbours next door and/or*
> *on the high seas, in prison or camp,*
> *hiding in a jungle of fear*
> *escaping with a hungry child*
> *needing a new life*
> *yearning for a return home ...*
> *they are here.*

The world has changed massively in the post-colonial era with its globalised market economy in which many unstable and poor countries fall victim to oppressive regimes. The consequent flow of refuges ensues. Sometimes the globalised, economic forces have contributed to the maintenance of the power held by oppressive regimes. The longest term refugees in the world are the Palestinians and the solution of the conflict causing their predicament is still far from view.

A Matter of Spirituality

The immensity of the refugee situation in our world can easily numb us in the West. The Christian is asked to face the topic in a particular way. Along comes Jesus and his message regarding 'the neighbour', a message that on the surface is ridiculously unrealistic: *anyone* in need is our neighbour. The world of first century Israel within the Roman Empire was big enough for the first believers at the time to begin thinking about Christ's way with 'the neighbour'. Now with our much larger world and its availability of instant information we face the question of how we can respond to this injunction with its immense proportions.

Immensity as a mental or analytical issue, with its question of how to meet the needs of so many needy people, is actually not the primary issue facing us. Immensity as an emotional and spiritual issue is; that is, response of heart and hand is what is primarily required of us. We access this level of response to the issue of 'the neighbour' when we choose to enter into stories of 'the neighbour'. The story *par excellence* is the one that Jesus told, the parable of the Good Samaritan. What happens to us when we genuinely enter into the events and feelings of this story? … of the Samaritan who stopped when the religious passers-by did not … lifted the wounded man onto his donkey … took him to an inn and paid for his rest? What stirrings arise in us? What fears and aspirations?

Immensity on any level of our being can and does paralyse us into a fearful position whereby we then take no action. However, when we enter the stories of the 'the neighbour', whether on the turf of sacred text or the shared space of storied encounter with a person in deep need, often we can find a way to hold our fear, to be aware of it and at the same time focus more on the other person and the events of his or her life.

This is a matter of spirituality – of prayer and contemplation, of honesty and humility, of sharing and communion, of acknowledging when the 'chips are down' in our un-neighbourliness. As we get to know more that fear is a strong emotion in each of us, we realise that it has the power in fact to cripple us and our choices. Then it is that we need to ask the Holy Spirit for help to find the way forward.

The spiritual way forward, however, is rarely simple. Enter defensiveness, a creeping 'them and us' mentality and the forms of justification that murmur to our inner ear that really there are so many other things to attend to – in the family and the local community; this is all a part of the culture of fear that holds court within us.

Naming these emotional elements within us is an important exercise to undertake for when they are objectified, then they can be properly looked at. They can begin to loose their negative grip on us as we find spiritual strength to make gospel-based choices.

At the same time there is the spirituality of intention and vision to cultivate: 'I will seek out and find a refugee community or those who work with them in order to en-flesh my concern. I shall no longer distance myself or allow myself to be distanced'.

In the 'Easter Journey' opportunity is often provided for participants to be exposed to situations of disadvantage and sometimes to spend time with refugees or asylum seekers. Again, it is the telling of stories with genuine listening that facilitates not only encouragement for the teller but also an invitation to cross boundaries of understanding and to make connections for the listener.

In the incident named at the start of this chapter we see an interesting aspect to the cross-cultural friendship that evolved. The older Australian woman who befriended the young refugee would have heard some translations of her life story by her husband in the 'Journey' group to which they belonged. But the far greater level of connection between the two women was non-verbal, intuitive and tactile. Here is an example of the importance of relating cross-culturally in more than words: my sensitivity to another person as my neighbour involves the whole of my senses and can be responded and related to with the whole of my being.

Target Action

In the early years of the twenty first century Australian society gained a fortress mentality about boat people and asylum seekers. Some of those who resisted this tendency decided regularly to visit the detention centres in our nation where many refugees were detained long-term. They found it a life-changing experience. They listened to the stories of those they sat with and heard about the texture and terrain wherein so much was lost and left behind. Friendships of support grew within a political environment that prohibited the refugees from rightful release into the community. The visitors to the detention centres found themselves in a predicament with their new friends that oriented them to the long haul of accompanying them and being advocates of their rights.

Turning to the refugee neighbour who is in need, is always for the long haul. Very soon we see that the engagement is both personal and political. For the supporters of asylum seekers and detainees the long haul in political terms frequently becomes a matter not only of protesting against one's own government's policies of injustice but also of developing an active concern for the countries from which the refugees come.

Supporters of detainees and asylum seekers and of other refugee groups and communities therefore find themselves in target action whereby they focus on one community and usually not more. They find there is so much to learn within the one culture of a community. In this way, slowly, degrees of effectiveness are achieved and the earlier sense of the overwhelming immensity of the problem is channelled down to a specificity of concrete or tangible engagement. Awareness of the many and varied needs of refugees from other countries becomes understood as 'a solidarity of commitment' with them.

My realisation of this last perspective on the refugee neighbour hit me at an annual festival of the Karen people in Melbourne some years ago. The Karen leaders invited many Australian-born people and most importantly among them a representative of the aboriginal community who gave an address and played the didgeridoo. In addition, some fellow refugee groups were invited who also contributed in the proceedings. Here was an expression of solidarity. The struggles shared were similar. The estrangement from home and land, the encounter with armed aggression and the need to maintain the richness of indigenous culture ... when these were shared a feeling of mutual strengthening was created. To be involved solidly in one group is enough, for with that engagement there can arise an outlook of solidarity with other similar groups.

For congregations or church groups target action is an effective method of involvement.

In this discussion I have not yet touched on the dimension of neighbourliness in the Christian perspective that is to do with how we, the apparently more advantaged, are affected. So much is received from sharing or working alongside refugee communities. The strength of community bonds rarely seen now in the West, is the first characteristic that strikes the welcomed visitor in the refugee's domain. The next gift from these communities is the simple humour that they share: a love of simplicity and with it, laughter. Then there is the storied faith, expressed within various religious traditions, that in time is opened up and which traces the refugees' journeys. Frequently they only survive by means of trust and encounters with grace, expressed in one way or another. These strengths are then interlaced with the rich culture and history of the people, as music, dance, story and symbol are expressed and seen to be so firmly and naturally embedded in their common life.

As westerners observe and become privy to the various expressions of the community life that they encounter, they realise how privileged they themselves are to know these people and how poor in comparison much of their own culture is. It is indeed a receiving of gifts which in time can be integrated into their own lives. And more especially the friendships that develop find a lasting quality.

68 The approximation of the number of refugees in the world as 20 million is defined as those who had fled to other countries from their own. Those who are refugees within their own countries is estimated at 80 million.

CHAPTER 15

INTER-FAITH ORIENTATION

Group Incident:
On Christmas Eve the local imam came to the church to light a candle for peace. A couple of group members present were fascinated by the gesture. They asked, "What did parishioners present think of the gesture? Does Christianity and Islam have much in common?"

After September 11 2001 many inter-faith groups sprang up in local areas especially for dialogue between church and mosque adherents. Embarking on the inter-faith journey is quite different from any other religious enterprise. The reactions of many Christians can be quite varied when they first attend an inter-faith group: either they feel strong disagreement about a belief presented from another religion or they are thrown back by what is presented into a serious consideration of aspects of the Christian belief, maybe for the first time. Both reactions raise the issue of the need for listening across the frontiers of the great religious traditions and of beginning to gain a measure of understanding.

Local inter-faith groups often started to meet under the banner of developing mutual understanding *in order to build peace in the community*. For many of the church people involved this endeavour of making a commitment to inter-faith dialogue would have been unimaginable a decade ago. Yet many Christians are beginning to be convinced that it is a vital part of living their faith. This chapter explores what is at stake in the holding of this conviction, a conviction that has the potential to "fascinate" those who attend the 'Easter Journey'.

Dialogue and Encounter

Two levels of interaction are always present in a good inter-faith group: one is dialogue – the exchange of ideas and experiences, and the other is encounter – the sensing of 'the other' through the ritual forms presented, the use of language, the rhythm of interaction, silences and the fellowship and friendships that develop.

The 'Easter Journey' trains participants in the disciplines of dialogue and encounter. In the process of listening to other group members with their stories and of responding to gospel text they acquire an approach to 'the other' not as 'stranger' to be feared but as 'neighbour' to befriend and through whom there is something to learn. Such a training can form the basis for dialogue and encounter in the wider context of inter-faith concerns.

For those who have participated in inter-faith sharing over a few years dialogue and encounter immerse participants into a 'sea of discovery' on three inter-related levels: valuing, learning from the other, and learning more about one's own religion. Participants find this shared journey to be humbling and at the same time dignifying of each tradition.

i. *Valuing*. Usually we start with an attitude of *tolerance* towards the other religion, a quality that is double pronged. It can show itself as doubtful, a reluctant type of tolerance or as open tolerance that is willing to learn. Both forms of tolerance can be in a group. Moving forward with a healthy form of tolerance by means of listening and exchange moves towards gaining *mutual respect*. Each discovers that the other religion holds dignity, is rich in tradition and produces genuine devotion in the believers. From respect a further step is made whereby the group members begin to *value* the tenets and perspectives of the other religion. Valuing is noteworthy for the capacity it holds – for those who take this third step – to appreciate beliefs that are actually contrary to one's own. This quality of inter-faith participation is the ground for potential, genuine peace-building in any conflicted context.

In an increasingly conflicted world the grass-roots learned capacity for inter-faith understanding that proceeds from tolerance to respect and then to valuing is indeed salt and light.

ii. *Learning from the other*. My own experience of this dimension of inter-faith activity includes the following example. The conviction that God is almighty is fundamental to Muslim belief. Among the ninety-nine names of God submission ("Islam") to the greatness of Allah holds a central position in practice. Reverence and obedience become the path to follow, as indicated in the command to pray five times a day. Observing this in Islam made me think of the way in which much of western Christianity has tended to domesticate God, rather than maintaining a true sense of awe.

In recent years I have had some conversations in Thailand with Buddhist monks. In the past I had difficulty seeing that reincarnation was in any way credible or even imaginable. Some degree of comprehension and with it a sense of respect, came to me more by way of encounter than dialogue. It was in relation to the spiritually detached but not unfriendly demeanour of the monks that pointed to, and were consistent with, this tenet of belief. I realised that reincarnation fits both within the context of the Buddhist core practices of mindfulness and detachment, as well as within the monastic culture in which the doctrine is held.

iii. *Learning more about one's own religion.* Inherent also in inter-faith sharing is learning more about one's own religion. I remember on the Sunday after Christmas in the sermon, reflecting on the mystery of the incarnation, and indicating that for the Muslim God becoming human is impossible. Had we ever thought about this view-point? ... Are we happy to see the incarnation as ordinary or natural? ... Or does this conviction stir us into wonder, deeper reverence and commitment? It was through inter-faith sharing that the danger of a taking-for-granted tendency in my own religious tradition has been alerted.

The personal discovery is made in this learning process that the valuing of another faith does not diminish one's own but mysteriously enriches and strengthens it. This way of proceeding includes the breadth of experience whereby a contrary view is presented and with a degree of comprehension can be appreciated, respected and valued, not in a moment but in a process entailing the sorting out of one's own response to beliefs foreign to one's own.

Mission and Peace

Two possible outcomes emerge for the Church in this exciting, challenging enterprise as it finds itself in a very changed world environment, an environment we have described as the end cusp of Christendom, a religiously interactive, pluralist world. One possible outcome is to do with the nature of Christian mission and other is to do with peace. They are best posed as questions:

1. Given the open-ended character of inter-faith activity – that is, we are not sure where it is headed – how can we

speak of Christian mission in this context? (in relation, for example, to the Great commission: "Go into all the world and teach … ")

2. Is there a potential contribution regarding peace-building and peace-making that possibly can be detected as an outcome of inter-faith activity for the wider community and world?

In relation to the first concern here it is the Vatican that has led the way in naming inter-faith activity in a positive light. In 1965 Pope Paul VI wrote *Nostra Aetate* ("Our Times") in which he affirmed the place of the other religions in the wider scheme of the divine plan. Each of the world religions warrants the respect of Christians. The following paragraph on Islam reads now as prophetic:

Since in the course of centuries not a few quarrels and hostilities have arisen between Christians and Muslims (we urge) all to forget the past and to work sincerely for mutual understanding and to preserve as well as to promote together for the benefit of all mankind social justice and moral welfare, as well as peace and freedom.

Pope John Paul II was also keen to see inter-faith understanding enhanced especially in the cause of peace. The celebration of a World Day of Prayer for Peace on October 27, 1986, when the Pope prayed not just with other Christian leaders but with leaders of the world religions, each praying in their own way and in silence together for peace in the world, marked a new stage in relationships between Christians and other world religions. Never before had an event such as this taken place.

The book *Transforming Mission* by the South African missiologist David Bosch is considered by many to be a very authoritative and comprehensive text on Christian mission in our times. In it Bosch goes to lengths in attempting to discern the place of inter-faith understanding in the context of mission. He comes to the conclusion that an open-ended approach, committed to the Holy Spirit constitutes the path that lies before Christians. He examines the much discussed approaches of the last century:

> *– exclusivism, that we must preach the Gospel to those of other faiths,*
>
> *– fulfilment, that by means of accommodating them and enculturating their traditions they will come to the light of Christian faith, and,*
>
> *– relativism, that all religions are culturally conditioned with each pointing to the one divine Reality.*[69]

Bosch argues that we must go beyond these positions. Encouraged by the dialectical thought of Karl Barth, he sees the way to proceed as one of dialectic with a basis in humility:

> *… both dialogue and mission can only be conducted in an attitude of humility … Christian faith is a religion of grace (freely given) and it finds its centre in the cross (which judges Christians also).*[70]

Apart from this theological premise on which to hang a perspective of inter-faith engagement Bosch adds that there is a need for an expression of repentance for the poor track record of Christians: "vicious intolerance by Christians was often unleashed on adherents of other faiths". In this regard he reiterates the note of humility:

> *… an attitude of humility is intrinsic to an authentic Christian faith … So, the word that perhaps best characterises the Christian Church in its encounter with other faiths is vulnerability.*[71]

To the outsider of inter-faith engagement this thinking may appear generally appropriate but questionable as to whether it can work or not. To those who are engaged in this approach, however, being "weak in order to be strong", as Bosch suggests, is indeed workable and, in addition, is found to bear fruit.

In response to the second question about peace-making and peace-building, time will tell. If the networks of inter-faith activity are sustained and increase, their effect could well be palpable. Western governments are becoming increasingly interested in the potential of networks for building regional and national inter-racial and inter-religious harmony.

The topic of moral values often arises in inter-faith discussions. The topic is readily connected to the furtherance of peace. A book released in 2006 by Madeleine Albright, *The Mighty and the Almighty*, is concerned to raise the question of moral values in relation to foreign policy. She notes that many in the Arab nations, whilst opposed to policies of terrorism, are not categorically opposed to all that Al Qaeda presents. What they concur with is the sharp critique of western values. The American administration's propagation of its version of freedom obscures this necessary area of debate. The critique that the West has developed excessively individualistic and permissive values is not simply a call to a return to a form of Puritanism, but rather it is a view that sees the personalised trend as bound up with apathy and irresponsibility on the social and political level.

A Muslim or western critique along these lines has not yet been heard widely. Madeline Albright's book is for popular readership and could be one contribution in the commencement of a creative, urgently needed endeavour. Inter-faith perspectives as they emerge locally and more widely inevitably move into areas of moral values (family, neighbour, community, responsibility, forgiveness, punishment, etc.) and it becomes clear that values in all religious traditions are bound up with their respective tenets of belief.

History and Tradition

In the area of Muslim-Christian relations there is a kind of subterranean stream of wholesome relatedness that has taken place between the two great monotheistic faiths over the centuries; this has existed despite there having been "not a few quarrels and hostilities" (*Nostra Aetate*, quoted above). Consider the moments of chivalry that occurred during the Crusades in contrast to the carnage, most notably in 1187, when Saladin liberated Jerusalem from the Christians after their occupation. Saladin let the Christian population leave unharmed yet the Christians 88 years before butchered the Muslim and Jewish inhabitants of the city. We can note the shared, cultivated civilisation of Cordoba in Southern Spain in medieval times. Or the writings of Muslim, mystical poets and authors like Rumi who greatly honoured Jesus, as indeed the Islamic faith does centrally as one of its great prophets.

The following story, told in Louis de Berniers' historical novel *Birds without Wings*, paints a fascinating inter-faith scenario. Set in a town in the early 1900s century in what is now southern Turkey, the Ottoman Empire was facing its declining years. Christians and Muslims are described as living in harmony centred around mosque and church, served by an imam and Greek Orthodox priest respectively. The people mix socially together. The imam, Abdulhamid, is a stately, learned figure and much respected, especially as he rides around the town on his tall horse, Nilufer.

There is a dramatic scene which illustrates the kind of dynamics that can occur when the two traditions live side by side.

THE IMAM KNEW THE BIBLE (AND THE KORAN)

A wealthy Muslim man of the town Rusten Bey has evidence to believe that his wife Tamara has committed adultery. In his anger he drags her by the hair into a public place. A crowd gathers instantly as he pronounces her offence. The casting of stones begins and crescendos as a corporate act of "gleeful cruelty and malevolent barbarism." Unnoticed, Abdulhamid approaches

> *riding into the midst of the crowd and roars, "Who is responsible for this? By what authority is this?" Rusten Bey steps forward and indicates he is responsible, declaring that his wife is an adulteress. "Don't you know the law?" replies the imam. Then he pauses suddenly and sees that there are Christians present who clearly have joined in the fury.*
>
> *"Do you know the prophet Jesus of Nazareth, peace be upon him? Well, do you? ... Go and ask your priest what the prophet Jesus said when he prevented the stoning of an adulteress ...* [72] *Father Kristoforos will tell you what you ought to know already. Go, and do not condemn yourselves any further."*

The narrative continues with the imam discovering that there were not four witnesses of the claimed act of adultery, as required in Islamic law. He commands Tamara to be taken to his house to be cared for and then he turns to Rusten Bey and says "See what you have done in your wickedness and ignorance" pointing to Tamara on the point of near death, and then adds before riding off, "You have a wound on your arm, you ought to see to it."

It is good to acknowledge the subterranean historical stream that carries a light of hope for Muslim-Christian dialogue and encounter. The stream does not need to be romanticised but nevertheless reconstructions such as this story can be encouraging as they address the realities of the time.

69 Bosch Orbis 1992 pp.478-82.
70 p.484.
71 p.485.
72 John 8:1-11.

IV.

LIVING WATER

Being the Baptising Community

Moving Forward

In this book I have been concerned to emphasise the significance of 'the searcher' – the many people in western culture who are wanderers, who are open to having a variety of personal and spiritual experience but without an anchor. I have also been keen to focus on baptism as an 'awesome rite' which, as I have outlined, is classically a part of a communal process and has its 'moment' at the festival of Easter.

In gathering up the experience of those in recent years who have trod this way I have offered reflections on what some aspects of the Christian life might look like in the future, particularly when and if the Church moves more deeply and intentionally into its nature as the baptising community. In the previous section therefore I undertook an exploration of six areas:

- letting the biblical 'Story of God' penetrate more into the life of faith and inform particular situations – Ch.10 – Well of the Word
- seeing sin and evil more with God's eyes as intermixed and coming to know Christ's healing in relation to these negative forces – Ch.11 – What on Earth is Sin?
- finding a way into the mystery of silent prayer and stillness – Ch.12 – Accessible Contemplation
- accompanying a few others at depth – Ch.13 – Spiritual Friendship
- engaging a world where the needy stranger is close at hand and where we can share significantly with those of other faiths – Chs.14 & 15 – Refugee Neighbours and Inter-Faith Orientation.

Other directions may come to mind as being potentially relevant for the future of the Church – such as the environment, the family, sexuality, health issues especially HIV/Aids, and so on.

What is offered is not to be regarded in any way as the consummate priorities of the Christian life but rather as an exploration and extension of the threads and currents that emerge from edge-centre faith journeying. These six directions in their own way do, however, point to the breadth and depth of the Christian life, to focuses which in the past many of us in the Church may not have chosen to emphasise. It could be said that we have tended to be content with a mild and moderate 'middle area' where there are fewer risks and where there is a sense of human security.

As Christians seek to move forward with a strong vision of baptism we need to *grow* baptismal consciousness in our faith communities (Ch.16) and *deepen* the vision (Ch.17).

CHAPTER 16

GROWING BAPTISMAL CONSCIOUSNESS

It has been the character of the edge-centre dynamics inherent in the adult initiation process that has given rise to these explorations. If, therefore, the Church becomes more oriented to the edge and adopts the process widely we can expect more clarity and dynamism about what constitutes the Christian life in the future. Social witness as we have seen in the last section (especially Chs.14 & 15) is an integral part of what is involved in the Christian way and further attention will be paid to this topic in the next (last) chapter.

Growing baptismal consciousness in the Church is the topic of this chapter. This form of consciousness is about growing a keen awareness to engage searchers or inquirers and ourselves with them in a rhythm of making connections between persons, God, the Church and the world with the outcomes of faith, ministry and enriched community. In order to grow this consciousness we must address the following:

- holding the vision
- making shifts in priorities
- taking stock of the present
- learning from other mission contexts.

Holding the Vision

Three elements come to mind in the light of the discussion to date as the way to hold together a vision of the future in which baptism returns to its rightful place within the Christian community. We can call these elements *cusp, culture and colony.*

Cusp is simply the acknowledgment that we find ourselves, in history, on the end cusp of Christendom. It implies that we have to begin to see and do things differently. It is a time of experimentation but in the midst of the experimenting stands the core requirement to look discerningly at baptism and to open up the sacrament into an adult journey of faith discovery as the developing norm of its practice. In earlier chapters I have drawn parallels with the fourth century, the beginning cusp of Christendom. We cannot do things the same way as then. For example, we have seen the sense of authority in society is different between then and now. At the same time, the way the Church then led people to baptism raises similar challenges for us now.

By referring to *culture* we acknowledge that the Church must always relate to cultural forms and must find ways to enculturate the Gospel without compromising it. Equally, the Church needs to find ways to challenge and stand against the wrongs in the culture. Christendom according to Hauerwas and Kreider (Ch 2), enculturated the Church in many ways that compromised Christian life and witness. In our own time we are therefore thrown into the task of discerning what the authentic Christian community way and witness is.

The word *colony* is a word Hauerwas uses to define what, he argues, the Church needs to become:

The Christian colony (of the future) is not primarily about togetherness but about individual call, communal call ... What sort of community (for example) is required to support ethics of non-

violence, marriage fidelity, forgiveness and hope as these are sketched by Jesus' Sermon on the Mount?[73].

In other words, our times require the Christian community to become more distinctly the ek-klesia (the Greek word for church, lit. – "called-out"). Hence the Church according to its nature is to have a living social witness in each generation.

As church congregations begin to see themselves as distinct from society they see the need to be prepared to give an account of their faith. People need to make the transition from affiliative (belonging) faith to owned faith (Westerhoff); in other words, believers need to move beyond being members of the local church as a person who simply belongs, to knowing what 'my faith is' and being "ready to share the hope that is within you." (1 Peter 3:15).

If these three components, cusp, culture and colony, describe the broad parameters of the vision for the future for us to hold regarding baptism, then the way forward involves filling in these parameters with content.

A fourth 'c' needs to be included in holding a vision in order for it to have content. This 'c' stands for the Catechumenate, the 'Easter Journey', as the form of adult initiation. At a conference on Christian initiation in Canada in 1991 Robert Brooks listed succinctly the following characteristics of the place of the Catechumenal process in the life in the Church:

1. *It challenges the Church to an awareness that the pascal mystery is the very centre of its life.*
2. *It develops a prophetic faith to challenge the values of society.*
3. *It challenges the view that baptism is an innoculation of the individual against sin and evil.*
4. *It challenges the compartmentalization and fragmentation of parish life.*

5. It challenges the Church's understanding of ministry.[74]

Making Shifts in Priorities

Effective support for local leaders who hold the vision becomes a major priority. Close support groups allow the dream of authentic initiation to be vitalised so that leaders can take heart again in the face of recurring resistance and know together that progress does take place albeit as slow. One priority for visionary church ministry today therefore is a commitment to leadership support.

Another priority is one that John Westerhoff names: local church leadership needs to move from a model of pastoral care, administration and education to a model of conversion and initiation. This transition takes considerable time and energy since the legacy of the Christendom 'habit' in which the first model is deeply embedded, is difficult in practice to transcend. It can only be achieved with the holding of a strong vision and having effective support.

Here we may need to clarify what the difference between an educational focus and a focus on initiation is, since at first sight both involve learning and formation in relation to the Christian faith. As Paul Dalzell puts it:

Education forms the character of those who are being educated within the context of a largely given identity. On the other hand, initiation aims at changing a person's sense of who they are.[75]

Once the transition has been inaugurated on the local level, shared ministry that is apostolically geared becomes a major focus, Local apostolicity is to do with being oriented to outreach of the searcher, to the poor and the vulnerable. Outreach opportunities that 'speak a word in season' in the local community in relation to what is happening in people's lives, raises the thought that the Church may in fact have something to say. Outreach of various kinds becomes a major strategy in order to gather people for the journey into faith and commitment as well as being avenues of community care in and of themselves. Another approach is simply being watchful in daily community contact in order to ask people to inquire and bring their questions.

The place of separate communities of faith outside the local church or parish is an issue the western Church is now facing. These new communities must be full expressions of church wherein baptism and eucharist, ministry, outreach and service are present. The internet can help grow alternative church clusterings but not hopefully as virtual faith communities. Nor can there be homogenous communities in terms of gathering like-minded people of one socio-economic or generational class. Not to meet face to face as church or not to have plurality in any gathered faith community – both of these options appears to be inherently anti-gospel. The emergence of *Contemplative Fire* as an alternative form of Christian community in England has the signs of being an exciting expression of church.[76]

Taking stock of the present

Taking stock is a significant enterprise in these 'cusp times'. In seeking to maintain a vision of the place of baptism in the life and mission of the Church there is in practice a spectrum of decisions made and practices implemented on the local level. This variety reflects the 'cusp' times in which we live. We do, however, have to bear in mind the seriousness of the fact that western culture can no longer support the growth in faith of many baptised at a young age (Ch. 2). Attempts to justify the on-going practice of near indiscriminate infant baptism without a strong form of engagement of the family before and after is becoming increasingly unjustifiable.[77]

Parish decisions about infant baptismal policy are usually made in order to prepare families for the sacrament, introduce them socially to the church community and follow them up after baptism. Different parishes come to different decisions about the use of the Thanksgiving Service for the Birth of a Child, either as an alternative offered to parents or as a preliminary occasion, possibly leading to baptism. Some parishes struggle to muster the human resources required for preparatory and follow-up ministry. Ensuring that the font is prominent and uncluttered at the rear of the Church, symbolising the entry point into life in Christ, is important to maintain. There is the need to revive total immersion as fundamental to the sacramental act and if it is deemed unworkable, at least to administer a generous pouring of water.

Clearly, in the Church of the early twenty-first century there is a spectrum of baptismal practice that takes place from parish to parish in relation to the request of parents for the infant rite. To illustrate, let me refer to the contrasting policies of two colleagues who are parish priests. Both are cathechumenal practitioners in their local settings; each represents different sides of the spectrum. One argues that infant baptism of non-committed parents is out of the question. Pastoral care, a Thanksgiving service, time spend with the parents encouraging them to join the 'Easter Journey' and inclusion in the round of invitations to various events in parish life … this are the recommended parish's strategy of engaging nominal parents who come with a request for baptism.

The other colleague suggests an unusual approach at the other end of the spectrum. In his parish he performs infant baptism simply on the basis of a request from parents and at the same time invites them to dinner to be held a week after. Baptism is normally celebrated in the main Sunday service. Some parishioners are also invited to the dinner. The logic of this approach is that many parents are not open to listening or participating in any form of preparation beforehand: they are blinkered with the intention that they simply want "Jimmy" done! They are only open to any engagement by the Church after a warmly communicated baptismal service. The practice to date is bearing some fruit.

It is also true that frequent celebrations of Holy Baptism of nominal families as 'fly by nights' in the main Sunday service, can be a way of confusing the regular congregation in their growing baptismal consciousness. The practice of the quarterly baptisms, often seen in the American Episcopal Church, commends itself in this regard.

Considering these and others relevant issues, it is important that parish leaders regularly talk over baptismal policy both within and beyond the parish, situated as the Church is in these 'cusp times'.

Learning from Other Mission Contexts

"Baptism is everything" was the comment of the emerging leaders of a Christian community among the Mesai people, as described in Vincent Donovan's book *Christianity Rediscovered*.[78] What brought about this seemingly exaggerated statement?

The way of conversion in some other contexts from our own can have much to teach us about Christian mission in our own context. Here let me take up this one quite celebrated example.

The missionary work of Donovan among the Mesai in the mid 1960s was an exploration with Mesai tribal communities into 'who God is in their culture'. It led to an introduction of the Gospel into that culture without preconceived notions of what the Gospel is. It was in the encounter of the Gospel with the culture that conversions gradually occurred. One village, after a series of discussions, refused the Gospel. But the other tribal groups with whom he worked felt led by the "High God" of Abraham to move forward into a relationship with the Christian God. This God was seen as the God who brought about peace by the sacrifice of the elder, Jesus. As a warring people, more than one year had to be spent on the topic of "the love of enemies." Then, after some years, the time came for decision and commitment.

The years of evangelism were an exploration into what it meant to live as a Christian community. As the time for baptism approached Donovan and the tribal leaders realised that to be baptised meant they then could baptise others. Gifts in the community were recognised, especially regarding those who had the gift of being evangelists. They were ready to move into being a eucharistic community in which all is offered to God. In other words, baptism entrusted them with everything in term of becoming a responsible church community with its own leadership to be ordained to the task.

Donovan was following the strategy of the Apostle Paul in setting up new churches. Soon after the celebrations of baptism were performed it was time for him to leave.

I provide this outline of this Mesai story because it points to the all-embracing nature of the meaning of baptism. The nature of baptism actually includes the dialogue of culture and faith in a movement towards conversion and sacramental immersion, in order then to live in Christian community. The community that baptises needs to ask similar questions to those that the Mesai asked: Who is God in our faith community? Who is God in our surrounding local – and wider – culture? What are of particularly striking qualities in the gospel narrative and teaching that need to be pondered in the local context? It is the communal discerning of the answers to these questions, especially in an edge-centre manner, that brings light to moving forward in openness and gospel-bearing engagement of the surrounding world.

To sum up, it could be said that to take the step of growing and acting upon baptismal consciousness involves a kind of "breaking sigh". The effort amounts to breaking into a territory that our deeper Christian selves somehow recognise as good and as the rightful place to be. It is new and different but connects us more authentically as Christian people with the "roll and surge" of the sea of the world around us. These images are inspired by the following short poem:

Steady sea roar
rises to wild hill
fills the dark house
with sound on salt air.

The woman stands naked
at the window –
her lover sleeps nearby.

She knows the sea,
its roll and surge.
She has ridden the waves
to the breaking sigh
on the wet shore.[79]

73 *Resident Aliens* p.77.

74 David Holeton (ed.), *Growing Newness of Life, Christian Initiation in Anglicanism Today*, Anglican Book Centre, 1993, pp.81-83.

75 *Four Shifts in Mission*, a paper given by Paul Dalzell at a Conference on Mission, Melbourne, 2005, in which he presented four shifts: from education to initiation, from belonging to owned faith, from Eucharist centredness to pascal mystery (baptism and eucharist) and from characteristics to a process by which Christians are made.

76 See the website www.contemplativefire.org

77 Daniel Stevick in his book *Baptismal Moments, Baptismal Meanings* (Church Hymnal Corp. 1987) is writing in the context of American culture, I think it is unpersuasive in attempting to see some legitimation of the continued practice of a traditional practice of infant baptism whereby there can be minimal contact with the family of the baptised.

78 *Christianity Rediscovered, An Epistle to the Mesai*, SCM 1982.

79 A poem by the Australian poet Janet Howie, *Rotation*, Janos Press 2004 p.18.

CHAPTER 17

PLUNGED INTO LIFE

'Taking the plunge' in the Christian sense can allude to risk taking in the communual, social and political life of the world in which we live. It is consequent upon taking the plunge into the waters of faith and new life. In the previous chapter we saw that there is another meaning associated with what is the title of this book. This is to do with local churches being prepared to 'take the plunge' into entering the stream of the initiation way with adults. That stream is about taking the risk, by intentional and strategic means, of offering people the riches of the Christian gospel.

The plunge that is the topic of this final chapter is about evolving social witness that arises from the heart beat of the Gospel received in community. In the increasingly fragile environment of global living we need to attend more courageously to this direction and not continue to carry with us the accustomed compromises of Christendom's habits that so readily have diminished the focus of core gospel values.

This social witness and its accompanying values for discipleship, as we have seen, have their basis especially in the teachings of Jesus in the Sermon on the Mount, summarised in the Beatitudes that begin the Sermon. We recall that his teaching here is about:

peace-making and "turning the other cheek",
mourning over the state of the world and the plight of the poor
mercy living
intimate depths of prayer with *Abba*, Father
thirsting and striving for justice
deep compassion grounded in bonded relationships …

We glimpsed in Chapter 2 how this was lived out in the early centuries of the Church.

The vision of a renewed and discipled Church that is pictured here amounts to detecting a communal future in which all 'the plunges' that have been described proceed hand in hand. It will be difficult, for example, to evolve strong social witness without the centre-edge dynamic of the initiation way.

Throughout this book we have pursued the way of initiation, as adapted from the early centuries, in order to enunciate what needs to be offered in our time. I hope that I have indicated my own excitement about the process, and the excitement for it of a growing number of others around the world in various Christian traditions. In the first chapter I pitched this excitement by referring to a poem that expressed the enthusiasm surrounding baptism in the early centuries. It does not read as a piece of poetry that lies dead and buried in history but rather it holds a lively relevance for the present.

The poem gave expression to how the process of adult conversion and baptism powerfully work together in a faith community setting in our own time.

Baptism, despite a person's age, is to do with being "reborn in these depths" and it "spits out youth", not according to the fantasy of modern culture that dreams of maintaining the superficiality of physically attractive youthfulness but rather, according to the spiritual energy of being made new in Christ.

In this final chapter a note needs to be struck regarding what characterises the truly initiation-oriented Church among the currents of the early twenty-first century world. How does 'baptismal enthusiasm' spill over into the guts and grist needed for discipleship in our world? And at the same time can be found to be grace-bearing? The centre-edge dynamic of the initiation way, as we have seen, introduces those of both the centre and the edge to the surprises of grace, as they learn to take risks in the following of Christ. It breathes into hearts and bones a 'can do' mentality in the Church and in society. In our western context Christian action will be to dare more than we have seen in recent generations, to dare more by way of simplified life style, commitment in prayer, works of justice and non-violence.

Apocalyptic Perspective

I can turn to no other emphasis than that of the apocalyptic dimension to strike what is the key note here. The word 'apocalyptic' is used in two ways in common speech today. It is used broadly in our culture to refer to the life threatened predicament of the planet and of humanity that is evident in the capability of nuclear and chemical weapons, in the threat of terrorism and in relation to global warming and environmental degradation. Apocalyptic in this sense means that we are facing the potential for self-annihilation in parts or across much of our globe.

Its other use is in the Christian sense that refers to the 'unveiling' – literal meaning of apocalypse – of the last days. According to the traditions of interpretation within the mainstream churches and their theologians, the question of whether or not we live now in an historical proximity to the End of all things – as divinely determined – cannot actually be discerned. Only the Father knows the day or the hour (Mark 13:32). Nevertheless, among the mainstream, I am one of those who argue that a certain apocalyptic stance is required for authentic Christian life today.

I am not thinking here of the primitive, banner waving, bill board carrying, "Repent for the end is near" outlook that is commonly associated with apocalyptic thinking, but rather with the more mature type of understanding that belonged to the early centuries of the Church.

The outlook of the early centuries regarding the End-time believed that God is ultimately in control of world events even in the face of social and political and, for the current world, environmental crises. Mature apocalyptic is a form of paradoxical thinking that believes in God's purpose yet knows that without the eye of faith there is little perceived evidence of that purpose manifesting itself. Equally, it is the form of thinking that acknowledges the graphic imagery of the last things in Scripture and responds to them in terms of urgent action and witness in the present.

The 'Easter Journey' introduces participants to a strong sense of expectancy. Through listening to each other's stories, witnessing the breakthrough of inner healing and conversion and being touched by the remarkable word in season of Holy Scripture, expectancy becomes a part of one's being or faith life. The apocalyptic dimension, when introduced, becomes a naming of what participants already are acquainted with on the personal and communal level.

Paradox and mystery are of the nature of apocalyptic. Although mature apocalyptic thinking sits lightly with the literalness of its often bizarre imagery, it nevertheless needs imagery. Its character is actually best set forth in song, or symbol, art or poetry. The African American slaves sang their songs of faith and hope both as a longing for the full Reign of God to come on earth and at the same time for freedom in the course of this life. "Swing low, sweet chariot, comin' forth to carry me home ... ", "Deep river, I long to cross over Jordan ..." – such spiritual songs inspired the enslaved black communities to work for liberation and at the same time sustained a faith in the Second Coming of Christ. The songs were an expression of both longings such that hope expressed for ultimate deliverance didn't remove them from the struggle for betterment in the present but rather enhanced it.

This truer form of apocalyptic creates a pathway of humble yet strong believing in relation to the social realities at hand. I am amazed what a powerful, spiritual cord is struck in people's hearts when so-called Negro Spirituals are sung in present-day congregations.

Glimpses in the present of the fulfilment to come are recognised with this line of believing. These glimpses are seen in simple acts of kindness and of courage, of insight in testing circumstances and of clear awareness of the presence of the Spirit. Hence a kind of apocalyptic tension exists in which an uncompromised focus on freedom and justice, that is promised to come in its fullness in the End-time, is accompanied by liberating moments in the present. Furthermore, in terms of effort and struggle in human history, breakthroughs of justice for oppressed peoples occur, as they have for the black American communities. This is how the Reign of God that Jesus inaugurated, *is active*.

Other oppressed Christian communities, in addition to the African American communities of two centuries ago, have maintained patience, struggle and longing with a still-to-be-fulfilled orientation. In my own involvement with the Karen refugees from Burma, instanced a few times in this book, I have seen many examples of such hoped-filled struggle. The longing in practice always centres on worship, spirituality, fellowship and action.

There is a kind of double focus of prayer and commitment being spoken of here. We could call it a lived tension of a Now and Not Yet orientation to the future. In the 'Easter Journey' a taste of it is experienced in the months leading up to the Easter font. The baptismal worship of Easter, when celebrated as the climax of initiation, strongly portrays the perspective of the Now and Not Yet for the congregation, that is, of God's active presence in the community's worship on the occasion, as it carries and holds all the hopes and struggles of the group journeyers to that point. In turn, the hope for a New World to come is glimpsed and maintained in the resurrection-focussed worship.

Believing in the mystery of the End-time, with expectancy in the present, always give ground for hope. As we adopt this kind of thinking we discover the power of the signs of the End in the present ... at weddings and funerals, with the poor developing their communities, in the accessed silent prayer where an inner river of peace is found to flow, in freeing moments of the sharing of the Word, and so on ... These are truly "earnests" (Wesley's word) of the End. We come to know them as such, to rejoice in them and dare to be obedient to Christ and his Gospel ever more deeply.

The apocalyptic dimension rightly has its place and prominence in each generation but sadly it has not always been so. Indeed, after the fifth century and during most of the era of Christendom, this dimension of hope and imminence nearly disappeared. When it did briefly appear it was usually in a primitive, fundamentalist form such as millenarianism. When it is a healthy part of Christian consciousness it clearly enables strong, faithful response in the witness of pilgrim men and women. Due to envisioning, close at hand, the presence of the love, peace and justice of the Christ seated victoriously before them, beckoning pilgrims in hope and sustaining them in the power of the Holy Spirit, witness is urgently geared to the present, as their spiritual focus is directed towards the coming in fullness of the wondrous Reign of God.

White Robed

If then the apocalyptic focus is vital to the Christian life in our time, how then is this focus grounded in baptism? If baptism defines and launches the Christian life how is apocalyptic thinking included in the sacramental act? In this regard I shall now refer to the significance of the white robe in the baptismal rite.

The white robe of Holy Baptism is a signifier that the newly baptised have a foot in the door of the fulfilled Kingdom of God. As such they are called to a strong gospel witness. The robe cladding is one of three post-immersion symbols. The signing of the forehead with oil and the giving of a lit candle constitute the other two symbols and also are signs of hope for the newly baptised. Being clad in a white garment then is the third of the symbols that traditionally follow the sacramental act of water immersion.

The apocalyptic character of the baptised life is therefore emphasised in the white robe symbol. The colour white suggests newness of life in such a way that the newly baptised are now oriented to the End-time and stand on the threshold of its fulfilment in some kind of radical nearness. The robing alludes to joining the throng of the similarly robed witnesses or martyrs depicted in the Book of Revelation:

Who are these robed in white? …

They have washed their robes and made them white in the blood of the Lamb. (Rev.7:14)

The theme is magnificently portrayed at Ravenna in the Church of San Apollinare Nuova (5th century). Along the walls of the nave in grand relief are depicted on one side the male martyrs of the early centuries poised and walking towards the Kingdom of God and on the other wall the female martyrs of the early centuries in like procession. Robed in white, recalling their baptism, all are holding their martyrs' or witnessing crowns in their hands, to offer them and to caste them before the seat of the Christ, there to be "lost in wonder, love and praise". The scene is stirringly apocalyptic in the sense that the martyrs are oriented to the radical nearness of the fulfilled Reign of God. Viewers are drawn into the nearness to ponder their call and where they will walk in their witness. It is as though the scene is accompanied by the singing of the second century canticle of the Church, the *Te Deum*, which includes these lines:

> *"the glorious company of apostles praise you*
> *the goodly fellowship of prophets praise you*
> *the white-robed martyrs praise you."*

Christian apocalyptic vision is baptismal, for it starts with the purity of heart and spirit that the cleansing waters of the font grant and symbolise. The pure in heart will see God (Matt.5:3). The 'white-robed' members of Christ in every generation are called to join in witness with the throng, pictured in the final biblical vision of the book of Revelation. The vision of God is theirs and is to be ours too.

But, we may respond, what of the horrors of persecution that can eventuate through taking more literally the call of the Sermon on the Mount and the following in the present of a crucified Lord? Is not some of this discussion so far overly romantic?

It does need to be said that persecution and martyrdom inevitably become a part of the true witness of Christians in any generation. In the early centuries the death of Christians whose witness was to the point of shedding their blood was called "the second baptism" or "the baptism in blood". Persecution and martyrdom are not foreign to the life of the Church in recent times. A third of the Christians in the world in the late 1990s operated in secrecy for fear of extermination. In *A Cloud of Witnesses* the author describes that throughout the twentieth century an unprecedented multitude of men and women were martyred for their faith.[80]

Our present generation, including the potential dangers, hopefully is involved in a retrieval of a dynamic of this apocalyptic orientation. It will enable contemporary disciples to live more fully the fundamentals of the Christian life as exemplified in the Sermon on the Mount, namely, of being peace makers, of maintaining a fresh mourning for the state of the injustice and thirsting for its overcoming, of maintaining mercy, gentleness and purity of heart in the midst of all that opposes wholeness. These are Christ's avenues of social witness, to be deepened and extended in our time in comparison to that which has gone before.

Stanley Hauerwas, whose writings have been quoted earlier, regards this retrieval as a simple matter for Christians, for "they know about the end". They know, or are learning to know, of what I describe here as a more mature apocalyptic and not a primitive version. Taking the command to non-violence – "to turn the other cheek ... " – he comments:

Christians are free to work in a non-violent way because they know about the end.[81]

The close relationship or renewed radical orientation to the End-time creates a freedom, a recklessness of obedience. Hauwerwas adds:

Our ethic depends on living in the mercy of God. For us the world has ended because of the cross and so we live in the last days.[82]

Who would have thought that the mere donning of a white garment within the simplicity of the baptismal liturgy, holds such significance! Much is evoked in baptism. Authentic life in Christ, launched forth sacramentally, embraces the apocalyptic dimension. The glorious reality of the incoming Reign of God becomes more heart-felt in the present with this kind of sensing inscribed on the heart and mind. The reading of the several parables of Jesus about the promised joyous sharing in the banquet to come and pointed to in the eucharist, finds its way into a daily spirituality of commitment.

Examining the thought of Hauerwas and some other modern Christian thinkers like him, leads to the realisation that evangelism and social witness are inevitably intertwined. In the emerging Church, living more in the way of the Sermon on the Mount and speaking about the saving, liberating Christ will go hand in hand. Speaking of Christ will not have credibility without social witness unless the choice increasingly occurs to diminish the message and make it into a truncated Gospel of a marketed form of cheap grace.

Two forms of present enabling of social witness lie in our path. One is to listen to the voices of the modern-day prophets. The life and writings of Bonhoeffer still stand out clearly to many Christians as a form of witness we must attend to. And there are others whose witness needs to be prayerfully and collectively discerned and listened to.

Secondarily, the engagement of the Church's edge is a way of evolving social witness. This is the process, described in these pages, of allowing the inquiring edge to speak and to respond to the word of scripture with those at the centre (of the Church's life) and so together to learn with them. This is to follow Jesus' way and it is the way of initiation. As the explorations of renewed forms of Christian life in Section III indicate, the centre-edge avenue, it will be a key for developing shared social witness in the future.

It is worth noting in passing, that some contemporary scholars whose works could be regarded as prophetic, point to militarism in the West as an example of a social form of evil in our time. In applying the thrust of their work to the present socio-political situation, scholars such as Walter Brueggeman in his work on the Old Testament and Alan Kreider in his work on Church history, can be cited as writing prophetically.

Washed – with Food for the Journey

How then is discipleship sustained, couched as it is in the apocalyptic vision? How is the reality of grace, encountered in lively, shared group journeying and sacramental act, made available for the on-going journey? Jesus was baptised to take the journey to his sacrificial death. How does the meal he inaugurated on the night before his execution actually strengthen us – as spiritual food? What then is the relationship between baptism and eucharist? Aiden Kavanagh provides us with a general starting-point here:

> *In baptism, the eucharist begins, and in the eucharist, baptism is sustained. From this premier sacramental union flows all the Church's life.*[83]

As the climax to adult initiation at Easter, the new Christians participate in both baptism and eucharist, in one leading to the other. They are formed in the meaning of both as they experience them and especially as they engage in group reflection on the sacramental life after Easter.

How do both sacraments actually support each other and work together? What is the basic understanding of each in relation to the other?

The newly baptised adult is ushered into the regular celebration of the Church's life that focuses on bread and wine. The water bath leads to the gathering at table. Alexander

Schmemann writes:

The baptised have died with Christ so that they might partake of his risen life, and it is this risen life that the eucharist manifests and communicates in the Church, making her members into witnesses of the things to come.[84]

Of course the simplest understanding of the relationship of the two sacraments is that baptism is the washing, cleansing and entry into new life, and, eucharist is food for the continuing journey. Schmemann refers to the risen life of Christ as available in both sacraments. Believers enter into this life in baptism and are renewed in it in the eucharist, as food of grace to sustain and strengthen them for the journey of witness, a witnessing "of the things to come."

In the eucharist there is a foretaste of the coming feast of the Lamb at the End-time. There is the manifesting of a corporate movement of access to the Father in heaven. There is the re-energising of being embraced again with Christ's presence as the witnessing community here in pilgrimage on earth, involving our continuing dying and rising with Christ.

As we hold to the truth of the eucharist with a lively spirit, with reverence and joy in participating, a yearning to welcome and enable others to enter into Christ becomes important to us. As the word of scripture is broken open in the first part of the eucharist (Augustine's *audible* word) the people are revived and deepened in 'God's Story'. There is the progression to the breaking of the bread and the pouring of the wine (Augustine's *visible* word). Stirred by this celebrated mystery of which Christians never tire, it cries out to be shared. The desire arises to draw others into the covenantal relationship – for preparing and immersing in water of those who are looking for and discovering Christ and his way, consciously or sub-consciously.

The eating and the drinking find fulfilment in the splash and the plunge, and vice versa. The Church, being exposed in the celebration of both sacraments, becomes more and more initiation focused as the way of being church.

By way of parallel with traditional family life – in which the family still eats together – the sharing of a festive meal with its special family memories, honoured and retold, holds the strong desire for others to be born into the household inheritance. What joy there is when a new life arrives!

Baptism and eucharist are further related in terms of the rediscovery and deepening of commitment that believers can encounter. Sometimes experiences of the needy world around us that we bring to the eucharist can facilitate a renewal of commitment in service and prayer. The following story illustrates this point:

> DARE TO REACH OUT YOUR HANDS!
>
> *Phillis was a member of a group visiting the Thai Burma border on a study-tour that I lead each year. Most of the time is spent with the Karen refugees from Burma. This was her second visit. At a group eucharist to conclude the visit she reflected on what the sacrament now meant to her after being in a refugee camp a second time.*
>
> *"To reach out your hands to receive communion is to risk your life in God's service," she said. The courage and faith of the refugees, incarcerated for many years, had been deeply felt by her. Response in the eucharist, after this kind of encounter, can only be one of risk-taking and sacrifice in Christ, such as to deepen commitment.*

Expectancy in relation to baptism, symbolised in being white-robed has its parallel in the eucharist. The acclamation, "Christ has died, Christ is risen, Christ will come again" evokes expectancy. The place of expectancy in the eucharist has its basis in the New Testament, as in St Paul's teaching, " Whenever you eat this bread and drink this cup you proclaim the Lord's death until he comes" (1 Cor.11:26). The early Church's major eucharistic emphasis was on calling on God to "come quickly", to bring in the consummation of the age. Eucharistic communities were 'white-robed' in that they were apocalyptic in outlook and lifestyle, reaching out to welcome, form and baptise new converts.

The final point to be made here regarding the relationship between the two sacraments is to do with the development of a graced community character. The presence of newly baptised powerfully reminds us of the privilege of being a part of the grace in which we now stand. We stand in a living, communal, never-taking-for-granted outlook of shared faith, centred on the graced sacraments of new life. As each faith community undertakes the baptising of adults, sharing in the journey with them to the font, storied memories of these events and the persons involved, will become told and re-told as significant to the community and these will be a source of joy.

Spiritual friends who were 'white-robed' in baptism and stood dripping with fresh resolve and alight with hope – these now are a part of the eucharistic fellowship of new and older Christians who together look for and live faithful avenues of discipleship and witness.

Plunged

To conclude the whole thrust of this book and its inter-related themes, the icon of the baptism of Christ comes to mind. A copy of the icon has accompanied me throughout the task of writing. It is a small icon that stands on my desk. Meditating on it has been a form of encouragement and inspiration throughout.

As I pondered the icon I came across a sermon by the Anglican divine, Lancelot Andrewes, preached at Pentecost (Whitsun) in 1615 on the theme, "Baptism is an opening of the heavens above Christ."[85] In the icon, as in the scriptural testimony, the heavens are portrayed as opened above Jesus. Here, in this quotation, Andrewes is suggesting that in every baptism there is an opening of the heavens, a locating of a particular baptism within the baptism of Christ. What an amazing yet simple set of connections are here in this brief quotation. It is indicating that on the occasion of the baptism of a human person there is a spiritual drawing into the event of Jesus' baptism in the Jordan when the heavens opened. As Jesus' core identity was revealed by the voice from heaven – "This is my Son' – the person being baptised is exposed to this revealing and is incorporated into the life of Christ.

Andrewes is clearly echoing the strong association of any person's baptism with the baptism of Christ. This association is particularly evident in the tradition of the Orthodox Church.

To ponder the Orthodox icon of the baptism in the Jordan (see next page) can evoke much about adult journey of initiation and the faith community gathered around in the process and event of baptism. In the icon Jesus is fully immersed into the darkened hole or 'cave' of the river, the waters of the world's chaos. He comes exposed to the task, naked in the waters, indicating his total reliance on his Father in heaven. As he is plunged into the life of this world the heavens open, the Spirit descends on him like a dove and God speaks to say this is his servant/Son (Matt.3:16f). There is a trinitarian revelation of Jesus as Son and servant, now at work in the Spirit in the world, to bring Life to the world. Exposed to this revealing, the baptised person is plunged into the life of the darkened world with Christ in order to rise with him bringing Life to the world.

The icon depicts Jesus immersed in the waters as an act of submission and obedience. John the Baptist stands in position, reverently leaning forward, extending his hand to the head of

Jesus. The scene is reminiscent of Philippians 2: "Christ took the form of a servant ... and humbled himself to the point of death ... " Jesus' ribs are showing like those of an emaciated human, a reference to his subsequent path of obedience. As the chant of the Orthodox liturgy has it:

Wearing the form of a servant, O Christ, thou comest forth to be baptised by a servant in the streams of the Jordan, granting deliverance of ancient sin, and sanctifying and enlightening us.[86]

The Baptism of Christ
Russian, late 15th century

The discoveries and the personal healings experienced in the adult initiation process, as we have observed, are a part of the "deliverance of ancient sin, of sanctifying and enlightening", manifested and focussed in the Easter sacramental act. In many ways the companions are like John the Baptist in welcoming others to the waters of baptism – into 'in-Christ-ness'. The process awakens the realisation and faith that Jesus Christ has veritably joined in life's darkened ways and is committed to the redemption of all.

Returning to a contemplation of the icon, we see that Jesus' left foot is about to leave the darkened 'cave', expressing his readiness for the journey ahead, his witness in the world, leading to his death and resurrection. We are called to follow as witnesses in our own time. To be noted is the shape of the darkened 'cave'. It is depicted as a mandala. The 'cave', as mandala shaped, represents the world and as such is also a symbol of impinging glory. The mandala is depicted as well in the icons of Christ's transfiguration and resurrection. A strong axial symmetry in the icon functions to emphasise the glory surrounding the ministering Jesus. The baptismal path will lead to glory. Truly we are to taste glory on the way.

80 Susan Bergman, *A Cloud of Witnesses, Twentieth Century Martyrs*, Harper San Fransicso, 1996.
81 Hauerwas p.88.
82 Hauerwas p.90.
83 Kavanagh see p.106 f.
84 *Of Water and the Spirit*, SPCK 1976 p.117.
85 Kenneth Stevenson, *The Mystery of Baptism in the Anglican Tradition*, Canterbury Press Norwich 1998, p.8.
86 From Morning Prayer of the Orthodox Church: Office for the Baptism of the Lord.